ISBN 978-1-333-66937-9
PIBN 10533546

FB &c Ltd, Dalton House, 60 Windsor Avenue, London, SW19 2RR.
Company number 08720141. Registered in England and Wales.

For support please visit www.forgottenbooks.com

FOREWORD

This Method has been written not merely to add another to the long list of instruction books on the market, but rather as an attempt to present the subject in a more logical and practical manner, and, at the same time, to introduce a number of features which have not been covered heretofore, but which are of vital importance to the mandolinist of the present day and of the future.

Particular attention is called to the reading matter and to the cuts illustrating the various points, both features making this Method valuable to student and teacher alike.

The word "Method" implies a *system of study* or method of procedure, and the entire work has been planned with the idea of presenting every point and subject *as it is needed* and not before. For example, the usual "Rudiments of Music" are not given in a dry, didactic form at the beginning, but the subjects are introduced at the proper time, as they are needed, throughout the work. Another important subject is the *tremolo*, which, in the majority of Methods, is introduced at the very beginning, notwithstanding the fact that progressive teachers, virtuosi and modern authorities are agreed that the very nature of the tremolo (a rapid succession of down and up strokes), demands a considerable degree of freedom and facility in the slower and more measured strokes before the rapid and unmeasured strokes can be properly and smoothly done.

Attention is also called to the pages devoted to the other instruments of the mandolin or plectrum family—the banjo-mandolin, tenor or cello-banjo, tenor and octave mandola and mando-cello, since every mandolinist should know something of these instruments, and it is believed that this is the first work which has given them consideration.

Many of the Melodies and Studies have been given titles—a feature which detracts in no way from their utility, but which, it is believed, will give them an added interest. Book I has been designed to provide a thorough *foundation* and if some of the principles and rules laid down therein seem didactic or arbitrary, it must be remembered that they are for the purpose of *development*, and that some of them will be modified as the pupil advances in technical and musical development.

In preparing this Method, the works of all the greatest authorities on the mandolin have been consulted and studied, including those of Munier, Bellenghi, Branzoli, Christofaro, Mariton, Pietrapertosa, Marzuttini, Bertucci, Tartaglia, Francia and many other foreign authors, in addition to those of all the American authorities.

This exhaustive research, coupled with the author's extensive experience as a teacher and soloist makes him believe that this work covers the entire subject of mandolin playing in a most comprehensive manner.

The endeavor of the author to cover the ground in a complete manner has necessitated the devotion of considerable space to the development of the correct manner of playing popular and dance music of various kinds. At the same time, however, it is believed that a real love for the *best* in music and musical literature will have been instilled, both through the high ideals constantly held forth and through the many examples and excerpts from the works of great composers that the Method contains.

In points of procedure wherein this Method differs from those with which the teacher or player is familiar, the author begs a careful consideration and test of its principles before judgment is passed.

A condensed synopsis of the three following Books will be found at the end of this volume.

In conclusion, the author wishes to say that nothing in this Method is an *experiment*, every principle having been given that severest of all tests—long continued use in the studio, with successful and gratifying results, and it is hoped that teachers and students alike will derive as much benefit from the careful application of these principles as has the author.

NEW YORK CITY

ZARH MYRON BICKFORD

CONTENTS

A BRIEF HISTORY OF THE MANDOLIN AND ITS DEVELOPMENT

In tracing the origin of the mandolin it is necessary to go back to the time when the plectrum was first used on a stringed instrument (since the plectrum is the one distinguishing feature of the mandolin family, as compared with other stringed instruments of the present day), and this takes us far back into antiquity.

The best authorities are agreed that practically all European instruments originated in various parts of Asia. An Egyptian painting discovered a few years ago on a tomb on the Eastern bank of the Nile, is said by Sir Gardner Wilkinson (an eminent authority on the customs of the Ancient Egyptians) to refer to the arrival of Jacob's family in Egypt. As one of the figures in this painting is depicted playing on a plectral instrument, we must assume that the plectrum on the strings was employed during the period of Joseph and Pharaoh, 1700 B.C. The Lyre, the first of the stringed species, was a great favorite of the ancients. According to the pretty myth, its invention is attributed to Mercury. The oldest Lyre, with three strings, was introduced into Greece from Egypt and was passed on to the Romans, by whom it was used as extensively as in Greece. There is a celebrated fresco at Pompeii representing two Lyre players, one of whom has a plectrum. The Roman *testudo*, the seven stringed Lyre, was used in Central and Western Europe at the commencement of the Christian Era. The Anglo-Saxons also possessed a form of the Lyre, which was generally or always played with the plectrum. The word plectrum is derived from a Greek word which means "to strike." Without doubt, the world's earliest inhabitants soon discovered that they could produce a louder tone by using a piece of wood, bone, or something of the sort, instead of the fingers in vibrating the strings. It is said by Alexander, the historian, that Olympus brought to Greece the practice of striking the strings with a quill. It has also been said by authorities that Sapho, the renowned Grecian poetess, invented the more modern form of plectrum, having carved one from ivory for her own use.

The *Nofre*, an interesting instrument, was a great favorite among the early Egyptians and Assyrians, some three thousand years ago. This instrument was similar in construction to the Tamboura (the mandolin of the East at the present time).

It is shown in representations of concerts of the 18th dynasty (B.C. 1575 to 1289) The Nofre affords proof that the Egyptians had made considerable progress in music at this period. The ancients knew and made use of the fact that a fretted fingerboard enabled them to produce any number of tones from a single string—a decided advance over all previous stringed instruments of the lyre and harp family. It is interesting to note in this connection that, so far as ancient records show, the fretted fingerboard preceded the smooth fingerboard, as exemplified in the violin family, by many centuries.

The Nofre had two or four strings and was played with a plectrum, the body being generally oval in form, sometimes with indented sides. This shows that thirty centuries ago man had already discovered that the tone of a musical instrument was greatly increased by the assistance of a "resonance box," or air chamber.

The Tambour or Tamboura, the modern form of the Nofre, is the favorite instrument throughout Egypt, Syria, Palestine, Turkey and other Oriental countries at the present time. The instrument has a long neck, with a fretted fingerboard, the frets frequently being made of "cat gut," the body being small and entirely of wood.

The strings are of wire and it is played with a plectrum. This instrument is said to have made its advent into Western Europe at the Moorish invasion of Spain, in A.D. 710—some form of it (most likely the Algerian Tambour, which greatly resembles the modern mandolin) having being brought into Italy when the Spanish, under Gonsalvo de Cordova, entered Naples about A.D. 1500. From this time, according to Italian authorities, the direct lineage of the modern Neapolitan and Roman mandolins is traced, they being the direct descendants of the Tamboura.

The earliest form of the Neapolitan mandolin differs in several respects from its present day form. For example, pegs were used to adjust the strings, in place of the machine-head, while the fingerboard ended at the twelfth fret, where the neck joins the body of the instrument, the additional frets being laid in the top or sounding-board. The E and A strings were of gut, while the D and G were practically the same as the modern strings.

For the perfected form of the Neapolitan mandolin we are indebted entirely to the inventive genius of Pasquale Vinaccia (1806–1882), who gave us every point of difference between the antique and the modern forms. It was he who remodelled and extended the fingerboard; introduced wire strings and substituted the machine-head. Italy is known to the present day as the home of the mandolin, and it is to this country that we are indebted for many of the masterpieces in its literature, as well as for many of its greatest virtuosi.

Strange as it may seem from the foregoing, the first instrument of the mandolin family to be introduced into America was *not* the Neapolitan mandolin, which has come to be the recognized form in this country as well as abroad, but the Spanish mandolin, known as the bandurria. This instrument was brought to this country in 1879 by a band of Spanish musicians from Madrid, calling themselves the Figaro Spanish Students, under the management of the famous impressario Henry Abbey.

This band of musicians toured the country and created a furore by their playing, many people believing that they played the mandolin. The bandurria or Spanish mandolin differs materially from the Neapolitan and flat-back models used in America and most other countries at the present time.

The shape of the bandurria is practically the same as the usual form of the flat mandolin, but there its similarity ceases, it being strung with six double strings, with an entirely different tuning from the mandolin.

Shortly after this organization gained fame in America, a number of Italians in New York who had brought their mandolins from Italy and played for pastime, but not professionally, seeing the success of the Spanish students, banded themselves together, taking the name of Figaro Spanish Students, and, adopting similar costumes, embarked on a tour of the country under the leadership of Carlos Curti, a well-known violinist.

The fact that this spurious "Spanish Students" organization used the Neapolitan mandolin and that they also made a great success, accounts for the erroneous impression which was prevalent regarding the instruments used by the original Spanish Students. After the return of the Figaro Students to Spain, the Italians, who had taken their name, disbanded and located in various parts of the country. Practically the only mandolins known to be in this country at that time were those belonging to these men and to other Italians coming here to locate. American tourists returning from Italy also brought mandolins to this country, as tourists have in more recent times brought the ukulele from Hawaii, with the result that the instrument soon became so popular that American manufacturers were obliged to meet the demand.

Mandolin clubs soon sprang up in various parts of the country and the instrument has experienced a steady growth, which is bound to continue.

England and America have been the chief sponsors for the flat model of the instrument, which is tuned and played exactly like the Neapolitan or classic model, and which is virtually the same instrument with a differently shaped body.

FAMOUS MUSICIANS WHO HAVE RECONIZED THE MANDOLIN

Some of the greatest composers the world has known have written for the mandolin. Handel, in his "Alexander Balus," accompanies the song "Hark! Hark! He Strikes the Golden Lyre," with the mandolin, in conjunction with other instruments. Mozart, in "Don Juan," used the mandolin alone for the elaborate and beautiful obligato to the most famous song of the whole opera—the "Serenade."

Mozart also played the instrument and composed two beautiful songs with no other accompaniment than that of the mandolin. These songs and the Serenade are included in a later volume of this Method. Beethoven also played the mandolin and wrote for it, one of his compositions for this instrument with piano accompaniment appearing in this work. Hummel, the great pianist, also played the mandolin and wrote a Sonata with piano and a Concerto with orchestra accompaniment for it. Later composers who have honored the mandolin in their compositions include Verdi, in "Otello," Boito in "Mephistofeles," Gustav Mahler in his Seventh Symphony, Wolf-Ferrari in "Jewels of the Madonna," Spinelli in "A Basso Porto," and Percy Grainger in a number of works. "A Basso Porto" had its first performance at Rome, in 1895, the King and Queen of Italy and the nobility of Rome being present.

While the entire opera was a great success, it was said by those present that "the most effective and taking number was the mandolin solo, written especially for the opera and performed by the celebrated mandolinist of Rome, Signor G. B. Maldura, accompanied by the orchestra, several encores having been demanded."

There are many other serious composers, both past and present, who have deemed the mandolin worthy of their efforts and this should furnish sufficient evidence that the instrument has a place among serious musical instruments and that it possesses an originality which cannot be duplicated by any other instrument when certain effects are desired.

"Why music was ordained?
Was it not to refresh the mind of man
After his studies, or his usual pain?
Then give me leave to read philosophy,
And while I pause serve in your harmony."

SHAKESPEARE.

SUGGESTIONS TO PUPILS

Select your teacher for his knowledge and ability, rather than for the cheapness of his rates, because the cheap teacher is always the most expensive in the end.

Ask your teacher to advise you in the selection of the best instrument you can afford—for cheap and unreliable instruments cause more failures in music than any other one thing—unless it be the cheap and unreliable teacher.

Having made these selections, follow your teacher's directions implicitly, confining yourself strictly to the work assigned

Under no circumstances attempt the tremolo until the preliminary work contained in this Method has been mastered.

Since music is an art for the ear and in no way concerned with the eye (except as a means to the end), from the first time the string is made to vibrate by the stroke of the plectrum, form the habit of *listening* to the tone you produce, never forsaking this habit in any degree, so long as you play this or any other musical instrument.

It is said that "practice makes perfect," but it must be remembered that it is only *correct* and *intelligent* practice which makes perfect. Any other kind is worse than useless.

Regularity and frequency of lessons is an important matter if you wish to attain the utmost efficiency. You should have at least two lessons a week, since the time you spend with your teacher is of more importance than all the time you spend on the instrument between lessons. Unless this suggestion is followed, you *cannot* make satisfactory progress, and you will have the humiliation of being outstripped by those who have studied only half as long as you have.

Be punctual at lessons, remembering that you have engaged the teacher's time, and that he cannot be expected to keep another pupil waiting to finish your belated lesson.

Missed lessons must not be the *teacher's* loss.

SUGGESTIONS TO THE TEACHER

Teachers who may have been accustomed to using the tremolo from the beginning are earnestly urged to give careful consideration to the system of right hand preparation, as given in this work. They will invariably find that students so taught will not only have a well-developed right hand for general purposes, but that the tremolo itself, when it *is* introduced, will come without an effort and in fact will be unconsciously conquered before it is encountered. The smoothness and evenness of this tremolo, as compared with that which is developed by immediately starting to *tremolo* is as glass compared to the teeth of a saw.

It is suggested that the teacher select suitable material outside this work, at frequent intervals, not so much for study as for sight-reading. The publisher of this Method has an excellent catalogue of music, suitable for all grades of teaching, ensemble and solo performance.

It is hoped that the teacher will continually call the attention of the pupil to the text-matter, which is of great importance.

It is also suggested that the teacher play with the pupil in the various duets for two mandolins, as well as in those which have an accompaniment for the guitar, for the stimulus it affords the pupil, as well as the aid it gives him in the matter of rhythm and tempo and the more pleasing musical result of the performance of his lesson.

Aside from this, the teacher should often play *for* and *with* the pupil the technical exercises and the various material included in all the Books, illustrating the various technical points, the phrasing, shading and general interpretation, not forgetting that the greatest teachers of all time, (past and present) and on all instruments have made this the chief feature of their instruction. Two of the very greatest were Franz Liszt, known as the world's greatest piano virtuoso (whose sole method of teaching was by illustrating at the piano), and the late Theodor Leschetizky, whose method was to sit at a second piano playing *with* the pupil and occasionally illustrating alone.

Munier, one of the greatest authorities on the mandolin and its music, said: "In giving the lesson, I find it an excellent system for the master to play *with* the pupil, the example thus given being very useful and compelling a gradual and exact development of the mechanism of the instrument."

1—Head
2—Keys and Pegs
3—Nut
4—Neck
5—Fingerboard
6—Strings
7—Frets

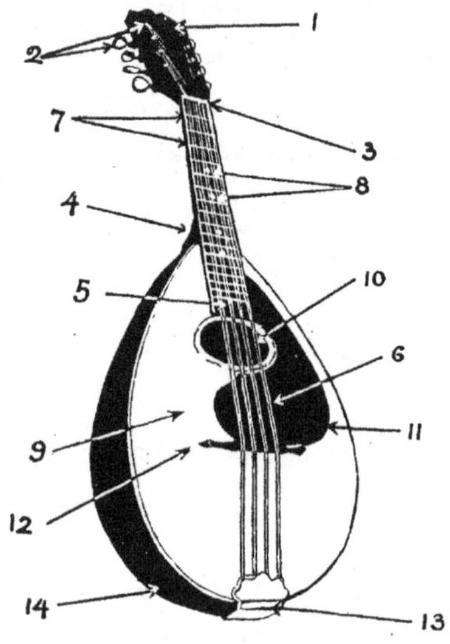

8—Position Dots or Marks
9—Sounding Board or Top
10—Sound Hole or Rosette
11—Guard Plate
12—Bridge
13—Tailpiece
14—Body

The position marks serve the double purpose of ornamentation and as an aid to the quick location of certain notes or positions. The opposite side of the instrument, not shown in the above cut, is called the Back, while the narrow strips glued together and forming the bowl of the Neapolitan model are called ribs.

DIAGRAM OF THE NOTES
ON THE FINGERBOARD OF THE MANDOLIN

The dots placed immediately at th left of the frets in diagram show the exact spot at which the fingers press the strings to produce the tones. The no es placed at the left of the lines indicating the frets in diagram are made at the frets - not at any place between two frets. The fret itself marks the exact location of the note, that is, the spot at which the finger would have to be placed on a fingerboard without frets, like the violin. The fingers must in all cases be placed close to the frets, as indicated by the dots. The number of frets on the average mandolin ranges from 17 to 20, while the ext nsion fingerboard gives an added compass of several notes.

Frets	E String	A String	D String	G String
Nut	E	A	D	G
1	E# F	A# B♭	D# E♭	G# A♭
2	F# G♭	B C♭	E F♭	A
3	G	B# C	E# F	A# B♭
4	G# A♭	C# D♭	F# G♭	B C♭
5	A	D	G	B# C
6	A# B♭	D# E♭	G# A♭	C# D♭
7	B C♭	E F♭	A	D
8	B# C	E# F	A# B♭	D# E♭
9	C# D♭	F# G♭	B C♭	E F♭
10	D	G	B# C	E# F
11	D# E♭	G# A♭	C# D♭	F# G♭
12	E F♭	A	D	G
13	E# F	A# B♭	D# E♭	G# A♭
14	F# G♭	B C♭	E F♭	A
15	G	B# C	E# F	A# B♭
16	G# A♭	C# D♭	F# G♭	B C♭
17	A	D	G	B# C
18	A# B♭	D# E♭	G# A♭	C# D♭
19	B C♭	E F♭	A	D
20	B# C	E# F	A# B♭	D# E♭
21	C# D♭	F# G♭		
22	D			
23	D# E♭			
24	E			

E or 1st String

A or 2nd String

D or 3rd String

G or 4 h String

NOTATION AND THE STAFF

Musical tones are represented by characters called NOTES. These are written on and between the five parallel lines comprising the STAFF, and, when necessary, on added, or LEDGER lines or spaces above and below the regular staff.

The following example shows the staff with the DEGREES (as the lines and spaces are called) marked.

The first seven letters of the alphabet are used to represent the degrees of the staff (also the syllables *la, si, do, re, mi, fa, sol* in some foreign countries), and the pitch of these degrees is determined by means of a sign called the CLEF, placed at the beginning of the staff. There are three Clefs in use at the present time—the Treble or G Clef ( ), the Bass or F Clef ( ), and the C Clef ( ), called the Alto (viola) or Tenor (cello) Clef, according to whether it is placed on the third or fourth line of the staff. The Treble Clef (used exclusively in mandolin music), fixes G on the second line of the staff, the Bass Clef fixes F on the fourth line, while the C Clef fixes C (middle C) on whichever line it is placed upon.

The following example shows the letters as they range themselves on the staff from the G fixed by the Clef.

clef note

g a b c d e f G a b c d e f g a b c d e f g a b c d e

The lowest G shown above represents the lowest note it is possible to play on the mandolin, the high E representing the other extreme.

The duration of a musical tone is indicated by the form or shape of the note used to represent it, the different forms being known as whole, half quarter, eighth sixteenth, thirty-second and sixty-fourth notes.

Since it is occasionally necessary to have pauses or periods of silence during the course of musical compositions, each of the above named notes has a REST, exactly corresponding to it in value.

The following table shows the forms of the various notes and rests, together with their values as related to each other. The *actual* value (in seconds), of any given note is always dependent upon the character of the music and the speed with which it is played, but the relative value, as compared to other notes of a different denomination and occurring in the same piece, never changes.

Notes	Rests
Whole Note	Whole Rest
Equals 2 Half Notes	Half Rests
4 Quarter Notes	Quarter Rests
8 Eighth Notes	Eighth Rests
16 Sixteenth Notes	Sixteenth Rests
32 Thirty-second Notes	Thirty-second Rests
64 Sixty-fourth Notes	Sixty-fourth Rests

HOLDING THE INSTRUMENT

The manner of holding the mandolin when seated is here illustrated. This position is usually preferable and is practically necessary when a violin or flat model instrument is used.

The right knee may be crossed over the left, though this is not absolutely necessary. If a bowl-shaped instrument is used, the back or ribs must be placed close to the body, well to the right side and with the top or face of the instrument very nearly perpendicular.

The lower edge may be brought out slightly, if desired, so that the fingerboard can be seen.

The left hand and neck of the instrument should be elevated slightly, as shown in the cut, but too much of an angle is not advised.

It will be found an excellent rule to hold the instrument so that from the tenth to the twelfth fret comes directly in the center of the body of the performer. The left hand must be brought well back, so that it is practically in a straight ilne with the right hand when in playing position, and so that the instrument is exactly parallel to the body. These rules must be carefully followed, as they are essential to the best results.

If the violin or flat model is used, the lower edge should be brought still farther forward so that the back of the instrument does not rest flat against the body. In all other respects both styles are held in exactly the same manner.

THE STANDING POSITION

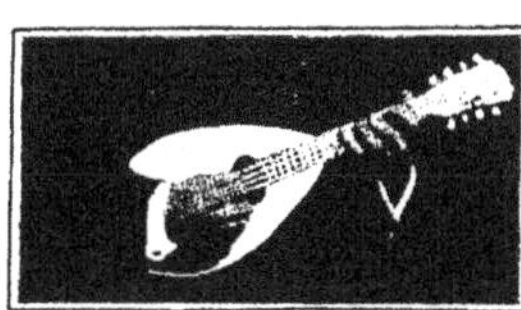

Many soloists prefer to use the standing position when playing in public. The correct manner of holding the instrument in this position is here shown. The general position is the same as when sitting, except that the back of the instrument must rest against the body just above the hip and the front of the instrument must be in a perpendicular position, with the upper edge brought slightly forward, if anything, in order that a firm grip may be had. As stated above, it is not practicable to play the flat model in a standing position, although it *could* be done with the aid of a cord around the neck.

THE LEFT HAND AND ARM

Since the left hand plays such an important part, both in the holding of the mandolin, as well as in playing, particular attention must be paid to its correct position. This hand should never *grasp* the neck of the instrument.

On the contrary, the neck *lays* easily just above the third (knuckle) joint of the first finger (*never* below it), while the side of the thumb, midway between the end and the first joint, is brought against the opposite side of the neck.

It cannot be stated too strongly that the thumb must always remain straight at the first joint, being bent *backwards* rather than in toward the fingers.

The tip of the thumb (when the hand is in the first position) should be in a line with the first fret. When playing on the first two strings, the tip of the thumb will barely show above the edge of the fingerboard and the ball or fleshy cushion will rest against the neck, but when the fingers are brought over to the third and fourth strings, the thumb turns slightly so that the side, near the corner of the nail, is the only part that touches, while the tip drops down to a point from the level of the fingerboard to a quarter inch below, depending on the length of the thumb. This slight change in the position of the thumb is caused by the fact that it is necessary to turn the hand when playing on the third and fourth strings so that the base of the fingers and the palm come very close to the fingerboard. The lower edge of the fingerboard must touch the first finger at a point very near the *second joint*, which means that the knuckle joint is brought well under the neck, thus *supporting* instead of grasping it.

The wrist must never be bent inwards, but forms a straight line from the elbow to the knuckle joints, with the single exception that when playing on the fourth string, it is frequently necessary to curve the wrist slightly *outwards*—the same being true in certain chord positions which will be encountered.

The arm must hang naturally by the side of the body, it never being necessary to throw the elbow out from the side.

THE FINGERS OF THE LEFT HAND

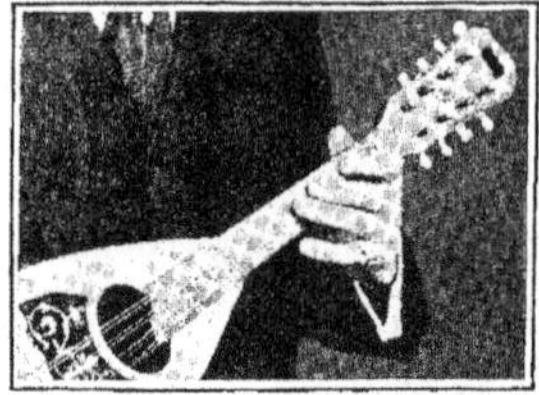

The action of the fingers must be entirely from the third joints, the first two joints being kept in a curved and stationary position

The tips of the fingers are used to press the strings, the nails being kept somewhat short so as not to interfere with the action of the fingers.

The accompanying cut shows the manner of placing the fingers on the strings, as well as the position of the thumb. In the cut, the first, second and third fingers are placed at the second, fourth, and fifth frets, respectively, of the third string, with the fourth finger held in proper position, either to drop to the sixth or seventh fret, or not, as the case may be, since this finger must always be kept in a line with the fingers being used, instead of being curled back in the hand or dropped below the fingerboard. This position of the fingers and particularly the fourth finger, is most essential and cannot be too strongly impressed on the mind. Particular attention should be paid to the position of the thumb, as shown in the cut, noting that the tip is below the top of the fingerboard and that the joint is straight. Careful attention to these seemingly small matters will have a very direct bearing on all future progress.

In order to develop a decisive action of the fingers they must not merely be laid on the strings, but must be dropped with a quick and forceful little blow, like the action of a little hammer. The finger tips must always be dropped close to the frets at which notes are to be made, touching the fret, instead of merely placed between the required fret and that preceding. This is essential to a good tone, although the mistake must not be made of placing the finger on *top* of the fret, since this would be as bad as to have it too far away.

It is also essential that fingers be left in place on the strings as long as possible, as in the case of ascending passages (playing toward the bridge), when the first, second and third fingers remain firmly in place so long as the playing is confined to that particular string. When the playing is transferred to another string, the fingers are all removed at the same instant. This is a most important rule and will be referred to very frequently throughout the work.

THE RIGHT ARM AND HAND

Unlike that of the violinist, the mandolinist's right arm must perform *two* functions—holding the instrument in position and manipulating the pick.

This double duty requires a more fixed and rigid position than when the arm merely draws a bow across the strings. The first consideration, then, is to hold the instrument firmly in place and this is done by bringing the forearm easily around the upper edge of the instrument, resting it just above and preferably against the tailpiece, at a point about midway between the elbow and wrist joints. It will be found that this position, aside from its being a perfectly normal and natural position for the arm to take, allows the hand to exactly balance the elbow and the rest of the arm.

This balancing is very important, since it relieves all strain and tension in the muscles of the arm and wrist and allows a freedom which can be obtained in no other way. After the arm has been thus balanced, if the mandolin is held well to the right, as previously explained, the natural weight of the hand will bring it down to the strings so that the pick will strike at a point about half way between the bridge and the end of the fingerboard and usually near the back edge of the soundhole. This is the normal position of the arm, wrist and hand, and must be strictly adhered to. With the mandolin and right arm both in the proper position, as explained and shown in the cuts, the question of keeping the wrist arched takes care of itself, since if it did not curve downward toward the strings, it would swing in mid-air.

The secret of maintaining this easy, graceful and normal position is to allow the elbow to hang and balance easily, rather close to the side, instead of raising it and holding it in a rigid position.

The general position of the hand and arm is shown in the cuts on a previous page.

THE PICK AND HOW TO HOLD IT

The pick or plectrum is very properly called the tongue of the mandolin, and its selection and the manner of holding it should receive careful attention.

In France the pick is called a *plume* and in Italy a *penna*, from the fact that some of the earliest picks were made from feather quills, somewhat resembling the old quill pens. Picks are made from a variety of materials, but best results will be obtained from celluloid, hard rubber or composition and tortoise shell. There are even more shapes and sizes than materials, used, but for general purposes the author of this work has found that a pick shaped like the subjoined diagram and of medium thickness, gives the best results.

For heavy or forceful playing a very hard and thick pick is best, but it is seldom advisable, under any circumstances, to use an extremely flexible pick. It is held by first partially closing the hand, as shown in the cut opposite, after which the pick is placed on the side of the first finger, at the first joint, with the point of the pick away from the hand and pointing nearly at right angles from the tip of the finger.

It should be placed far enough over the finger so that about a quarter of an inch projects beyond the nail.

The thumb is then brought down so that the ball or fleshy hump, exactly midway between the end and the first joint, touches the flat surface of the pick, thus holding it securely in position. The thumb joint, like that of the left hand, is kept in a straight, though not a *strained* position, while the remaining three fingers are held slightly separated and in exactly the manner shown in the second cut. The second joints of the first two fingers are separated slightly more than the rest, but the first joint of the second finger is curved sharply so that this finger crosses the first finger in such a manner that the bases of the nails are exactly in a line with each other and the corners nearly touch. The third and fourth fingers then fall into line in an easy and graceful manner, the little finger being a little farther out or more open than the others. A careful examination of the second cut will illustrate all these points, the importance of which cannot be overestimated.

When the pick and arm are held in the manner described, the point of the pick, when resting against the strings, will be found to point slightly toward the fingerboard from a perpendicular position. This slant must be *very* slight, however.

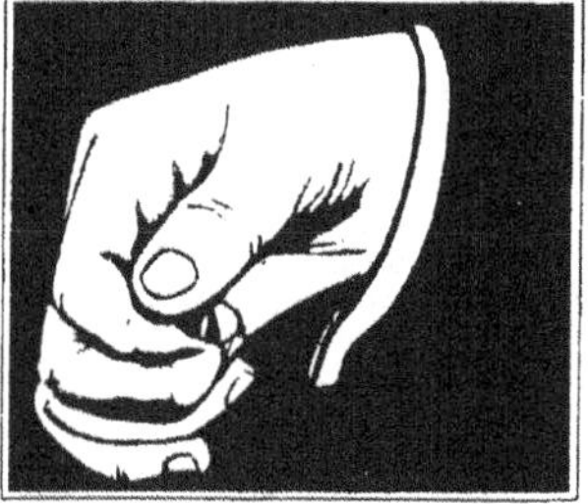

TUNING THE MANDOLIN

Since the instrument must be put in tune before it can be played upon, it is important that the ear be trained from the first to recognize both when it is *out* of tune, and what is of even greater importance, when it is *in* tune.

Each pair of strings must be made to sound exactly alike, or in *unison*, the unison strings always being spoken of as a single string. The following illustration shows the notes represented by the four open strings and to which they must be tuned.

The G to which the fourth string is tuned is the first G below Middle C on the piano, the D that immediately above this C and the A and E each a fifth higher, in succession.

TUNING THE MANDOLIN (Continued)

For the purpose of developing the ear it is well to experiment with each pair of strings, attempting to bring them to the same pitch if they are out of tune with each other, or to put them out of tune and then bring them back.

When tuning, both the instrument and right hand should be held in the regular playing position, the left hand being used to turn the pegs.

To test any two strings, the pick is held very lightly and pressed or pushed gently across them, not too quickly, in order to determine, first of all, whether there is a difference in the pitch. If there *is* a difference, no matter how slight it may be, for the purpose of the present experiment, the lower or outside string may be left as it is and the second of the pair made to sound exactly like it.

Before this can be done, it must be determined whether the string is too high or too low. Should it be too low, or *flat*, the peg to which the string is fastened is to be turned slightly so that the string is wound tighter on the peg.

In this connection it is well to see that the third and fourth strings (D and G) are wound on the pegs in such a manner that they lay *inside* the four pegs on the side nearest the performer. They should also be put on the pegs in consecutive order, that is to say, the outside G string on the first peg, nearest the body of the instrument, the other G string on the next peg and so on with the D's. With the strings adjusted in this manner, each string will be easy to locate and the pegs will always turn to the *left* to tighten or make them higher in pitch and in the opposite direction to make them lower. The A and E strings are also wound from the inside of the pegs, so that, being on the opposite side of the head, the pegs will be turned to the *right* (with the instrument still held in playing position) to tighten or make them *sharper*, and to the left to make them lower in pitch. The four strings on this side of the mandolin should also be adjusted consecutively, that is, the outside E on the first peg nearest the body of the instrument, and so on in regular order. The two important operations in tuning are, first to listen carefully to determine whether the string is too high or too low and then to listen just as carefully to determine when it is exactly in unison with the other.

In tuning, it is important that the pick glide gently across the two strings, always from the G string side. After having set the strings in vibration in this manner, the pick should not touch them again until after the peg has been turned, so that the ear may catch the final vibrations or waves as they die away.

This is a much less nerve racking process than to continually strike the string while it is being tuned. After the ear has learned to detect the difference in the vibrations, the instrument may be tuned to the piano or another instrument. This is done by first sounding one of the notes to which the open strings are tuned, preferably A, on the piano, pitch pipe or other instrument, and after the ear has thoroughly digested the pitch of the note, gently picking the A string nearest the D, by sliding the pick across it and dropping it *between* the two A strings. This will sound but one of the pair of strings and will prevent the vibration of the other. The ear must determine whether this A string is higher or lower than the note struck on the piano and the peg then turned, as explained above. After the string has been made in unison with the piano, the second A of the pair is then tuned to the first, in the manner described above. The other three strings can then be tuned to their respective notes in the same manner. After each pair of strings has been put in tune temporarily, it is advisable to stretch the strings by pulling or pushing very forcefully on them with the pick, for the same reason that the piano tuner "thumps" as hard as possible on the keys when tuning, and that the violinist pulls and stretches his strings, especially when new ones are put on. This method takes the "slack" out of the strings and makes them *stay* in tune. After this stretching the strings must again be brought back to pitch.

Another method of tuning is to get the A from the piano, as above, or from an A pitch pipe, after which the A string is stopped or pressed down at the seventh fret and the E strings tuned to the note thus made. This is done by first comparing them and then tuning the E next to the A string, after which the outside E is tuned to its mate.

The process is then reversed and the D string stopped at the seventh fret, the note thus made (A), being tuned to the open A string. The G string is then tuned to the D in the same manner—by being stopped at the seventh fret and this note tuned to the open D string. All the strings are tuned by first making one of them in tune with the next string or the piano, and then tuning the second of the pair to the first—*not* to the adjacent string or the piano.

Still another method is to tune by octaves. After having tuned the A string, as a starting point, the E string is stopped at the fifth fret, the note thus made being tuned exactly an octave above the A. The fifth fret of the A string is then stopped and the D string tuned an octave lower, after which the G string is tuned an octave lower than the fifth fret of the D string. It is suggested that this method be used more as a test, than as a regular method of tuning.

Still another method, and preferred by the author, is that employed by violinists, who of course do not have the advantage of frets by which to tune. This method is to get the A in the usual manner, from piano or other instrument, after which the inside E string (nearest the A) is sounded or "chorded" with the A, the effect being what is known as a *fifth*. If the E string is perfectly in tune, it is a "perfect" fifth, and if not, it must be made so.

TUNING THE MANDOLIN (Continued)

The outside E is then tuned to the other, after which the D string nearest the A is sounded with it (A), and the fifth thus formed made "perfect" in the same manner. The second of the D strings is then tuned to its mate, and the G nearest the D sounded with the open D. This is made into a perfect fifth and the other G tuned with the first. This is a much quicker method than any of the others, but requires a very accurate ear. It may be of assistance, when using this method, to think of the lower of any two adjacent strings as "do," or the first tone of a scale, the higher string being "sol," or the fifth of the same scale.

When the mandolin is to be played with the guitar or banjo, it is occasionally found desirable to start the tuning process with the G string, since this string has the exact pitch of the third strings on both guitar and banjo.

The subject of tuning has been dwelt upon at length for the reason that the author has found a lamentable lack of knowledge as to the proper method of going about the matter among mandolin players.

HOW TO USE THE RIGHT HAND

Now that the instrument is tuned, held in the proper manner, the right arm properly balanced on the edge of the instrument and the pick held properly, the next step is to actually *play*. Tones are produced on the mandolin by setting the strings in vibration by means of the right hand and pick, and upon the manner in which this is done depends the whole structure of mandolin playing. There are three fundamental and general movements of the pick—the down stroke, used consecutively—the down and up strokes, used alternately (each stroke making an individual note) and the tremolo or *sostenuto* movement, in which an attempt is made to sustain a single tone for a certain length of time, but in which no account is made of the individual down and up strokes required to make this tone. From these three fundamental movements are derived a considerable variety of strokes and styles of playing, but they never lose their predominating importance. The order in which they are named above is that in which they are to be introduced and developed, since it is the only logical manner in which they can be treated, owing to the fact that the second depends upon the first and the third upon the second.

THE DOWN STROKE

The cut on the following page shows the position of the right hand when it is raised, ready for the down stroke. The pick must be held very loosely and in such a manner that its flat surface, very near the tip, strikes squarely against the strings.

In making the stroke, the hand is dropped suddenly from the position as shown in the cut, so that the pick strikes the pair of strings and rests firmly against the next higher string, after having vibrated the required strings.

It is essential that this stroke be made with a quick and energetic movement of the hand and also that the tip of the pick rest against the adjacent string after the hand has dropped. The starting point of the pick when making the down stroke, in the early stages of practice, should be from two to three inches from the string and at a height of at least a half inch from a straight line drawn across and parallel with the strings. One of the objects of this slight angle from which the pick approaches the string is to allow the point of the pick to drop in between the strings so as to rest against the adjacent string. This could not be done if the pick struck the strings and crossed them on a line parallel to their level. On the contrary, with the pick exacly perpendicular to the strings, there would be the continual danger of striking more than one string.

In order to make the down stroke in this manner it is necessary to tilt the hand very slightly away from the body so that the pick points a very little toward the body, instead of being exactly perpendicular.

Another important feature of the stroke is that, while the little finger is raised with the rest of the hand as the stroke starts, it goes down with the hand so that the back of the nail touches the guardplate as the pick rests against the next string. It is also important that both pick and little finger *remain* at their respective resting places, with the hand and arm entirely relaxed, until the hand is brought back, just in time for the next down stroke.

When the down stroke is made on the first string (E), since there is no higher string for the pick to rest against, the little finger and even the knuckles of the second and third fingers are used to stop the downward swing of the hand.

The point of the pick should never touch the guardplate or top of the instrument, it being stopped in mid-air at a point no farther from the E string than this string is from the A string.

THE DOWN STROKE (Continued)

As previously explained, the back of the nail, or more properly, the side or outer corner of it, should be allowed to rest against the guardplate or top of the instrument as the hand drops toward the strings for the down stroke, and, during the early stages of practice, this finger should leave the top of the instrument when the hand is brought back to its starting point, ready for another down stroke. As the speed of the strokes increases, however, and the length slightly decreases, this finger does not leave the top, but glides back and forth easily, following the motion of the hand. In this connection, Munier, the great Italian authority, says: "The other fingers of the right hand (aside from the thumb and first finger) should be relaxed; the little finger should glide on the sounding-board and serves as a guide for making the tremolo." Tartaglia another eminent authority, also says: "The little finger should not be stuck fast to the sounding-board, but it must glide easily, following the movement of the hand." Pietrapertosa, the famous authority of Paris, also says: " . . . the little finger resting on the guardplate, but without force, for this finger, moving along the top, acts as a guide to the hand in the movement of the pick against the strings."

It has been the experience of the author that a very light contact of the little finger with the instrument serves as a guide for the movement of the hand, both in single strokes and in the tremolo. The single exception, when its touching might be a matter of choice, is when playing two or more strings with the tremolo, as in "duo" playing. While on the subject of down and up strokes, it should be added that the wrist joint does not move in the least when making the strokes, the entire motion being made by swinging the hand from its pivotal point—the middle of the forearm. This swing causes a rotary motion of the two bones in the forearm, but the wrist itself is held in a perfectly fixed, although *relaxed* condition.

THE DOWN AND UP STROKE

While the up stroke of the bow in playing the violin plays an almost equally important part with that of the down bow, the same cannot be said to be true with the up stroke of the pick. For example, two consecutive notes on the violin are frequently played with alternating down and up bows, no matter what their speed may be, while the same notes played on the mandolin would require an entirely different stroke from the right hand. The only definite rule that can be given at this stage is that notes which are played slowly are to be taken entirely with down strokes, while those requiring more speed than is convenient for consecutive down strokes must be played with alternating down and up strokes.

Since the up stroke is most often used immediately following the down stroke, it is suggested that a down stroke be taken, as previously explained, for example, on the G string, allowing the pick to rest firmly against the D string.

It should also be explained that, while about a quarter inch of the pick projects below the nail of the first finger, the only part that actually touches the pair of strings as the stroke is made, is the very point—less than a thirty-second of an inch. If the pick is held at the suggested angle, the projection of the point of the pick as it rests against the D string after the G string has been struck, will be but slightly more than the thirty-second part of an inch.

After having allowed the pick to rest for an instant, with all muscles perfectly relaxed, the hand and pick are brought back with a quick motion to the exact point from which the down stroke was started and following the very same angle or imaginary "groove," but touching the strings on this upward journey, the same as when the hand went down. If the pick is held very loosely, both strings of the pair will be vibrated when taking the up stroke, since the point of the pick will glide quickly across them, the same as on the down stroke. It is most essential that the directions for using the very point of the pick be carefully followed, especially in taking the up stroke and also that the pick merely rest between the thumb and finger instead of being gripped, otherwise the slight angle at which it is held will cause it to slip *under* the first string encountered.

This is disastrous, as it not only prevents striking both strings, but causes the pick to get caught under the string so that the stroke cannot be finished without an accident of some sort.

THE DOWN AND UP STROKE (Continued)

Should the second of the pair of strings occasionally be missed on the up stroke, it need cause no concern, since the two strings are always to be considered as *one*, and the missing of one of the pair is partly compensated by the fact that if the strings are perfectly in tune, the second will vibrate in sympathy with the first, and also by the fact that up strokes are, as a general rule, on *unaccented* or rhythmically less important notes than the down strokes. Many of the greatest virtuosos, soloists and authorities, both in this country and in Europe openly advocate the striking of but a single string on the up stroke. The author would suggest, however, the above method as being most nearly ideal.

When the tremolo on two or more strings is studied, the pick must necessarily strike both strings of the pair on the up as well as the down stroke, but the slight angle at which the pick is held for work on single strings ceases to be necessary at that time, since it would be inconvenient to always rest the pick against an adjacent string.

TIME AND MEASURE

Music is distinguished from unrelated and isolated tones by the grouping together of these tones in pleasing and rhythmical combinations. Rhythm itself is the "movement imparted by the alternating of accented and unaccented tones in regular order." This rhythm or regularly recurring beat is the underlying principle of all music and its development and constant application should be the first care of the student. For the purpose of developing and keeping this steady rhythm it is essential that the various Studies and Exercises be *counted*, preferably *aloud*, in the earlier stages of advancement.

This counting must not be done in a haphazard manner, suiting the counts to the difficulties or convenience of the fingers, but must be as precise and regular as the tick of a clock. It is suggested that, as a preliminary study for the development of a steady rhythm, the counting be done in connection with the ticking of a clock, the ticks which come on the *second* being taken as beats or counts.

In counting "one-two-three-four, one-two-three-four," the words should be spoken in a quick, energetic manner, the pulse actually being *felt* inside, like a heart beat.

Another method of developing a strict sense of rhythm, time, pulse, counting, or whatever name may be given it, is to actually walk about the room, making each step as decisive and regular as though marching to the music of a band. The counting is done with each step, as with the ticks of the clock, and in the same energetic, snappy manner—not drawling the words, but snapping them out with a strong impulse.

Tapping the foot lightly on the floor, or tapping with a pencil can also be utilized in the same manner. In all these methods the pulse must be felt and projected very strongly *mentally*, the physical motions being merely aids to the mental impulse or thrust. For the purpose of assisting the eye in reading music and showing the strong accents, the notes are divided into small groups called *measures*, these measures, like the inches on a yard stick, being of exactly the same length, *in seconds*, during the course of any particular composition.

The length and character of the measures or groups is indicated by the figures in the shape of a fraction, placed at the beginning of the staff, after the clef sign.

This fraction or Time Signature, indicates, by its lower figure, the kind of notes to be taken as the *beat* or *count*, and by the upper figure, how many of these notes are used in the group or measure. Thus the 4/4 in the following example shows that there are to be *four quarter* notes, or their equivalent in other notes or rests, to each measure. The letter C is often used in place of the figures 4/4, this being known as *Common Time* or measure. This particular time or measure is known in Italy as *tempo ordinario* (ordinary time).

The letter C is a modernized form of the semi-circle (( ) of the ancient "measured music," in which it signified the division of a whole note into two half notes, in contra-distinction to a certain kind of measure, formerly used, in which the whole note was equal to *three* half notes. The perpendicular lines crossing the staff and dividing it into measures, are *bars*, although the *measures* themselves are frequently, though improperly, called "bars" in modern usage.

The heavy *double bars* at the end are used to indicate the close of a piece or movement and also to indicate the division into sections of parts.

"*Keep time. How sour sweet music is when time is broke and no proportion kept.*"—SHAKESPEARE.

OPEN STRING STUDY.

The sign (⊓) over the four notes in the first measure indicates the *down stroke*, and these strokes are to be continued throughout the study. For the present, all *beats* are to be invariably played with down strokes. Every measure is to be counted, as indicated in the first—the quarter *rests* receiving the same amount of time as the notes, each count or beat lasting one second.

EIGHTH NOTES AND ALTERNATING STROKES

In this little Study the eighth notes are to be taken with down and up strokes, alternating, each pair of eighths requiring the same amount of time as a single quarter note. This exact division will be more easily accomplished if each "one-and," "two-and," etc., is compared to a word with two syllables—as "ta-ble," "ta-ble," while the quarter notes take up the whole beat, like the one-syllable word "chair."

Particular attention must also be paid to the manner of making the strokes, as previously explained.

Up strokes are indicated by the sign (**A**).

NOTES MADE ON THE G STRING

The notes between the open G and D strings (A-B-C), are produced by placing the left hand fingers at certain frets on the G string.

The cut shows the manner of placing the first finger at the second fret to make A. B is made by placing the second finger at the fourth fret, the first finger remaining in its place in the meantime. C is made with the third finger at the fifth fret, while both of the other fingers remain firmly in their places.

The frets are indicated by the figures over the notes, while the figures at the left of the notes refer to the left hand fingers.

The absence of a figure before G indicates that it is made on the open string, although the sign "o" will be frequently used to indicate open strings. The fingers must be used in the manner previously explained.

NOTES ON THE D STRING

The notes laying between the open D and A strings (E-F-G), are produced on the D string, E being made with the first finger at the second fret. The accompanying illustration shows the second finger placed at the third fret, for the note F. The first finger is shown in its place, on E, where it must remain while the other fingers are being used. The third finger is then placed at the fifth fret for G, both of the other fingers still remaining in place. In the section after the double bar, the fingers can only be left in their places on the strings so long as the notes *ascend* (toward the bridge). For example, the first finger remains on E (second note) while the next note, F, is played, after which both fingers are raised for the open string. In the case of the ninth note (E), the finger remains in place while the three following notes, G-F-E, are being played. This principle is important and must be scrupulously adhered to.

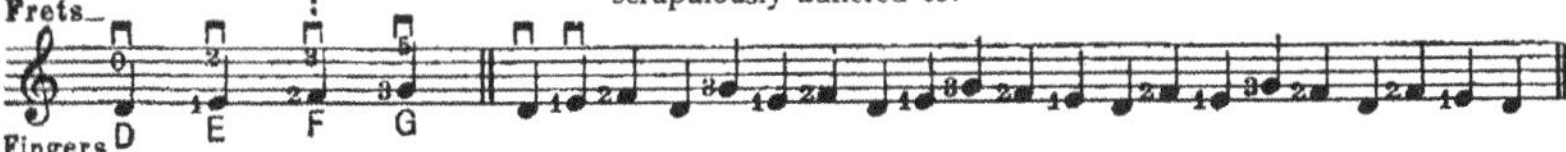

NOTES ON THE A STRING

The notes laying between the open A and E strings (B-C-D), are produced on the A string, B being made with the first finger at the second fret, C with the second finger at the third fret and D with the third finger at the fifth fret, as shown in the illustration.

In each case the fingers remain firmly on the string, so that by the time the D is reached, the three fingers are in place, as shown in the cut. It will be noticed that in this and the other similar Exercises the notes are not divided off into groups or measures. They should, however, be played as evenly as possible and invariably with down strokes, the up strokes being reserved for the second of a pair of eighth notes. Particular attention must also be paid to the manner in which the strokes are made, making them in the vigorous manner prescribed under a previous heading. These are invariable rules and *must* be followed.

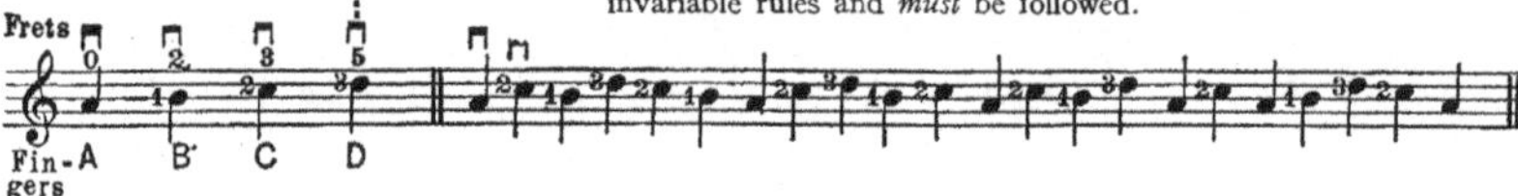

EXERCISE

NOTES ON THE E STRING

All notes above the open E string are produced on this string, for the present, at least.

This includes F-G-A and B, this marking the limit or extent of what is known as the *first position*—that is to say, that position of the hand in which the first finger plays or stops the *first note* or letter on each string, not counting the open string. Other positions, in which the hand moves higher up the fingerboard (toward the bridge), are explained in a later volume of this Method.

The F on this string is made by placing the first finger at the first fret.

This note will be found a little more difficult to make than the notes made with this finger on the other strings, but it is only necessary to close the joints of the finger a little tighter than usual, so that the tip rests against the first fret, the position of the thumb and the hand in general remaining the same as before.

G is made at the third fret, with the second finger, the first remaining on the F in the meantime. The third finger is placed at the fifth fret for A, both the first and second remaining in their places. It is now necessary to use the fourth finger for B at the seventh fret, as shown in the illustration. All the other fingers must remain in their places while this finger is stretched to the seventh fret. For the purpose of loosening the muscles and tendons of the hand and fingers and making them more pliable, it is suggested that the joints and the fleshy part of the hand at the base of the fingers be kneaded or *massaged* and also that the fingers be gently stretched apart by forcing the closed fingers of the right hand between each pair. Particular attention must be paid to the position of all the fingers and the thumb when making this B, as shown in the illustration, and the position of the thumb should be compared with that shown when the first finger makes the A on the G string.

Frets 0 1 3 5 7

Fingers 1 2 3 4

E F G A B

Exercise

E String

The Four Strings Combined

(Every finger must remain in its place until a new string is taken)

Study for Locating Notes

This Study is for the purpose of fixing the names and location of the notes thoroughly in the mind. It is suggested that it be gone through with once without the instrument, merely naming each note aloud. It may then be played, still naming the letters aloud, after which it should be played again, counting very steadily to each note. It is not necessary to play it rapidly, but it must be practiced so thoroughly that it can be played without any hesitation.

Should it be necessary to look up any of the notes, they can be easily located by the use of the table, just above. The names of the notes and the fingering have been purposely omitted.

Study in C

Melody

"One must not only learn to count while playing, but make the playing fit the counting." ANON

Amusement

(Employing all Strings)

Two Four Time or Measure

This kind of time, indicated by the fraction 2/4, is used as extensively as Common Time, and requires two quarter notes, or their equivalent in notes or rests, to each measure. The eighth note now takes on more the character of a beat note, being usually taken with a down stroke. 2/4 Time is usually counted at the rate of two quarter notes to the measure, the eighth notes, should there be four, being counted one-and-two-and. It can be taken as a general rule that all eighths are played with down strokes, the exceptions being in slow movements and when the tremolo is used. These will be referred to later in the book.

The eighth notes in the following Study are played at about the same rate as the quarters in previous Exercises.

Study in 2/4 Time

Sixteenth Notes

Sixteenth notes have exactly half the time value of eighths, hence are played exactly twice as fast. This means that they must be played with alternating down and up strokes, like eighth notes in 4/4 Time. It will be of assistance at the beginning to count four to each measure in 2/4 Time when the measures contain sixteenth notes, as they frequently do. This gives each eighth note one beat, the sixteenths being counted one-and, etc. The use of the eighth and quarter-rests is necessary in the last measure of the following Study, in order to complete the measure, since the note has but one beat.

Bingo!

The Tempo di Polka at the beginning means "in the time or style of a Polka," this being a lively Dance, always in 2/4 Time. The two dots placed just before the double bar at the end of the sixteenth measure are called "repeat dots" and indicate that the Strain (sixteen measures) is to be repeated. The dots occur again at the end of the piece, causing the last sixteen measures to be repeated.

"Let not a day pass, if possible, without having heard some fine music, read a noble poem, or seen a beautiful picture." GOETHE

Cherry Time
Polka

Keys and Scales

A KEY is a family or group of tones bearing certain fixed relations to each other and centering around a certain fixed tone or point of repose known as the key-tone or tonic and from which the key derives its name. A SCALE is a ladder-like progression starting from the key-tone and proceeding a degree or letter at a time until the octave or key-tone has been reached again, thus requiring eight tones to complete it, while a key is distinguished or made manifest by seven tones. Since a scale is merely one of the many compositions or melodies which may be built from the tones constituting a key, these terms must not be confused. Keys are called MAJOR and MINOR according to their character. The difference in the pitch between any two tones is called an INTERVAL, these differences or distances being measurd by means of STEPS and HALF STEPS (also called TONES and HALF TONES.)

The half step is the smallest interval used. All scales may be grouped under two general headings - DIATONIC, those progressing letter by letter, according to the alphabet, and CHROMATIC, those progressing entirely by half steps, thus making use of all the INTERMEDIATE tones (those coming between the regular tones of the scale).

The intermediate tones are represented by the aid of characters called SHARPS (♯), FLATS (♭) and NATURALS (♮), the last also being called CANCELS.

Half steps, or chromatic tones, are represented on the piano by the regular succession of black and white keys - every key, and on the mandolin and other fretted instruments by the regular succession of frets - every fret.

There are two forms of the diatonic scale - major and minor. A major scale requires whole steps between the first and second, second and third, fourth and fifth, fifth and sixth, sixth and seventh tones and half steps between the third and fourth and seventh and eighth tones. This order of progression must always be preserved and should be memorized, after which one can easily build a scale from any desired tone or starting point. There are two forms of the Minor Scale in modern use - HARMONIC and MELODIC. The Harmonic minor scale requires whole steps between the first and second, third and fourth, fourth and fifth, half steps between the second and third, fifth and sixth and seventh and eighth and three half steps (a step and a half,) between the sixth and seventh tones. The Melodic minor is the same as the Harmonic in ascending, with the exception that the interval between the fifth and sixth tones is made a whole step, which in turn makes a whole step from the sixth to the seventh. In descending, the Melodic minor calls for a whole step from the eighth to the seventh and the seventh to the sixth degrees, this in turn making a half step from the sixth to the fifth.

Below are illustrated the major scale of C, and the chromatic scale, showing the intermediate tones. The use of the sharp (♯) before a note indicates the tone between that note and the degree next higher. The sharp is thus said to raise a note a half step, its tendency or inclination being upwards. To be exact, it is impossible to raise a note or a tone, since they are stationary. What the sharp really does, therefore, is to represent the tone (also stationary) a half step higher.

The flat (♭) is used to represent the tone a half step lower than any given note or letter, its tendency being to lead downwards to the next tone a whole step away.

The cancel or natural (♮) is used to cancel the effect of a previous sharp or flat or to represent the tone indicated by the unchanged or "natural" note.

Chromatic or intermediate tones may be represented by either flats or sharps, as shown in the illustration.

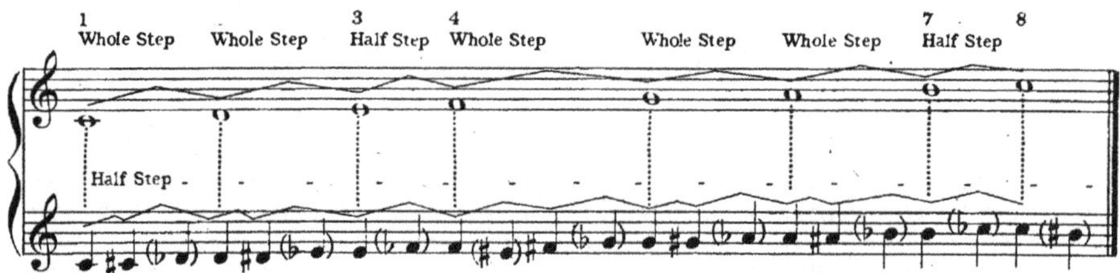

The word chromatic is derived from a Greek word and refers to the manner in which a scale progressing by half steps was formerly written, the sharps having been represented by red notes and the flats by yellow notes, the picture thus presented being a colored or chromatic scale.

Scale Exercise in C

In playing the high C (fourth measure), it is necessary to extend or stretch the fourth finger to the eighth fret, the other fingers, or as many of them as possible, still remaining in their places. In the following measure this finger is drawn back to the seventh fret for the B without being lifted from the string.

Each major scale has its relative minor scale-that is, one which is related in a harmonic sense and also in the matter of appearance or "family looks."

Thus it will be seen that the scale of A minor looks like the scale of C, except that it starts on A. In order to bring about the succession of steps and half steps in this scale, as previously given, it is necessary to make use of sharps for two of the tones in ascending, these being brought back to their natural position by the cancels in descending. When used during the course of a scale or other composition, these signs are called ACCIDENTALS. The Harmonic minor scale is the same both ascending and descending.

Accidentals are effective only in the measure in which they occur, with a single exception which will be noted later. The fourth measure of the following scale is an example of the effect of the cancel, while the same character before the F in the following measure is used as a reminder, rather than because it is necessary.

The sharped G's in the "Melody" must be carefully noted and played one fret higher than G (natural). It is also to be noted that sharped notes are always played with the same finger as the regular note. The low G♯, made at the first fret on the G string, is of course an exception to this rule.

Scale of A Minor
(Relative of C Major)

(SPECIAL NOTE) "Big Injun" and "At The Bridge" *(Bickford)* are suggested as recreations at this point. For Sale *By Carl Fischer.*

Melody

(Key of A Minor)

Key Signatures

There are as many keys as there are chromatic tones in the scale-twelve, and each of these keys is distinguished by a sign or signature, consisting of sharps or flats placed at the beginning of the staff, immediately after the clef sign. The key of C (and its relative-A minor,) in which all the Studies and Exercises have been thus far, is called the natural key, since no sharps nor flats are required to represent its tones, nor, on the piano, anything but the white keys. The scale of C is taken as a model or standard for all other scales, the same order of steps and half steps being followed, no matter what tone may be taken as the starting point or key-tone. Thus it follows that when the scale is started on G, it becomes necessary to sharp the F, in order to bring a whole step between the sixth and seventh and a half step between the seventh and eighth tones of the scale. This necessary change could be indicated by inserting the sharp before every F occurring in the composition, a method occasionally used during a temporary transition to another key, but the usual method is to place the sharp on the fifth line of the staff at the beginning, thus indicating that all F's, whether occurring on this particular line or on another octave (as in the first space,) are to be sharped, and that the scale or composition is in the key of G. It will thus be seen that it is very important that the key signature be carefully examined before a piece is played.

In the following illustration, the sharps are placed in parenthesis before the F's merely as a silent reminder.

Scale of G

Scale Exercise in G

(SPECIAL NOTE. A thorough understanding of the scales, and their constant practice at a later period of development is very essential and for this purpose all the scales, major and minor, have been grouped together in one of the later volumes of this Method, arranged in a form that will be found not only useful technically, but interesting musically.)

"I have never been in favor of the many automatic mechanical methods of producing touch. There is really only one real way of teaching and that is through the sense of hearing of the pupil." OSSIP GABRILOWITSCH

Foward! March!

(SPECIAL NOTE) "Daddy Longlegs," "Crystal Waters" and "Killarney Waltz" *(Bickford)* may be used here.

Scale of E Minor

(Relative of G Major)

This scale, having the same signature as G major, is called its relative minor, and, like the scale of A minor previously given, is in the Melodic form. The necessary accidentals must always be introduced in the minor scales. Whenever figures are placed before or over the notes it must be remembered that they refer solely to the left hand fingers and never to frets.

Study in E Minor

Dicky Bird Waltz

A Waltz requires the use of three beats to each measure instead of an even number.
This is indicated by the fraction at the beginning. The first beat or note in each measure is to be strongly accented (by striking more vigorously), so that the pulse or swing can be felt and recognized.

Sixteenth Notes in Common Time

It now becomes necessary to play and think of a group of four notes to a single beat or count, and this grouping can perhaps best be illustrated by the use of a four-syllabled word, like "of-fer-to-ry" or "cat-er-pil-lar," the first syllable very strongly accented, as is the first note of the group in playing.

In the same manner that it takes no longer to speak a word with four syllables than a word like "bird," so does the group of four notes take no more time to play than a single quarter note. In either case it is a single impulse or thrust. It is suggested that the counting be done as indicated under the notes-speaking the word very sharply, but mentally dividing it into the four parts or syllables. The mark (>) placed over the first note of each group is called an accent mark, and means that this note is to be given a very strong accent or emphasis. Attention is again called to the necessity of decisive and vigorous strokes, allowing the pick to rest against the next higher string, but holding it very loosely. This Study should be played as quickly as possible, for the development of the right hand.

Chords and How to Play Them

A chord is a union or combination of two or more harmonizing tones played together. In the following little Studies, the first measure and every alternating measure after that shows the preparation for the chords in the intervening measures.

The fingers are to be left firmly in their positions on the notes during each two measures. The short dashes between the down stroke marks indicate that the pick is to glide to and over the notes following the first, without being once lifted for another stroke. This manner of using the pick is known as the glide, the push stroke and the coulé. In one sense it is a continued down stroke, rather than a series of strokes. The waved line (⁐) indicates that the notes of the chords are played in consecutive order, from the lowest note up, but practically together, the pick being used exactly as indicated for the first measure.

It should be added that the vigorous swinging stroke is not used for chords, but rather a gentle caressing stroke.

(SPECIAL NOTE) "Harp and Cello," "Little Drum Major" and "Merry Moments" *(Bickford)* may be used here.

The Tremolo

The tremolo, as applied to the mandolin and other fretted or plectral instruments, is the name given to the movement which attemps to sustain, or imitate a sustained tone, as one produced by drawing the violin bow slowly over a string, or by holding down a key on the organ. The nearest approach that can be made to this sustained tone is the rapid reiteration of single short tones, and it is to the blending of these single tones into an approximate sustained tone that the student must apply himself, since a smooth, even tremolo is an absolute necessity in all artistic playing. There are two important reasons for having delayed its introduction until the present time: first, since the tremolo movement, considered mechanically, is nothing but a rapid succession of down and up strokes which must be played with the utmost evenness and regularity, it cannot properly be attempted until the right hand has gained considerable facility and is under full control in the slower and measured strokes: second, tremolo playing does not develop a strict sense of rhythm, although it requires it, therefore the rhythmical feeling must be thoroughly developed, by the use of single and more or less vigorous strokes, before the tremolo is attempted. For these reasons, the introduction of whole and half notes has been delayed, since they cannot be correctly played without the use of the tremolo. The author's experience has proven that it is best to make the acquaintance of new notes as they have to be played in practical work, rather than to learn to play them in a certain manner and then be obliged to play them another way later on. There is nothing in the use of the pick in tremolo playing, as applied to single strings, which does not apply and has not been repeatedly used in the previous work in single strokes, except that the length or swing of the strokes cannot be as great nor should the individual strokes be quite as vigorous or decisive. Everything else applies-the resting of the pick against the next string, the angle of hand and pick, the striking of the pair of strings in both down and up strokes, the looseness of the pick and the easy gliding of the back of the little finger on the top.

There can be but one rule given as to the number of strokes to be played to any given note - it must be an even number, that is, start with a down stroke and end with an up stroke. It is occasionally necessary to begin a tremolo with an up stroke, in which case this rule would have to be modified.

A definite number, as four, eight or sixteen strokes, should never be applied or thought of, in connection with notes of any denomination whatever, as this measured or rhythmical stroke does not make a tremolo.

The following Exercises are for the purpose of developing the regularity and speed of the down and up strokes and in their practice it is suggested that, instead of accenting the groups, the accents be confined to each new note or letter, as it is encountered, thus, in the first Exercise, accenting the first G only, making the succeeding fifteen notes a steady but unaccented string of strokes.

These studies are to be practiced until the strokes can be made very rapidly and very evenly - just as though they were being counted or measured, but without doing this. The abbreviations in the second Exercise do not indicate the tremolo, but merely that each quarter note is to be played in sixteenths, this being made still plainer by means of the four dots over the notes. This abbreviation was formerly used in mandolin music to indicate the tremolo, but never properly.

The following example indicates in a general way the continuous strokes of the tremolo, as it would appear to the eye. The only rule which can be given for the speed of the strokes in the tremolo is that they must be as rapid as they can conveniently be made without tightening the muscles, and when this Example is played in this manner the desired effect will be obtained - a sustained tone.

Whole Notes

As may be judged from the value of a quarter note, a whole note has the value of four beats or four seconds. It is known as an open or white note, as distinguished from quarter notes and those of shorter duration, which are called closed or black notes. The first practice on this Scale Study should be done by making a slight break in the tremolo between the notes, thus allowing a slight attack to be made with the first down stroke as each note is played. Afterwards it should be played with a continuous tremolo from beginning to end. Each of these whole notes is to be given four slow and regular beats, the right hand meanwhile keeping up its steady swing, without regard to the number of strokes. Left hand fingers must be left firmly in their places until required on another string.

Scale of G

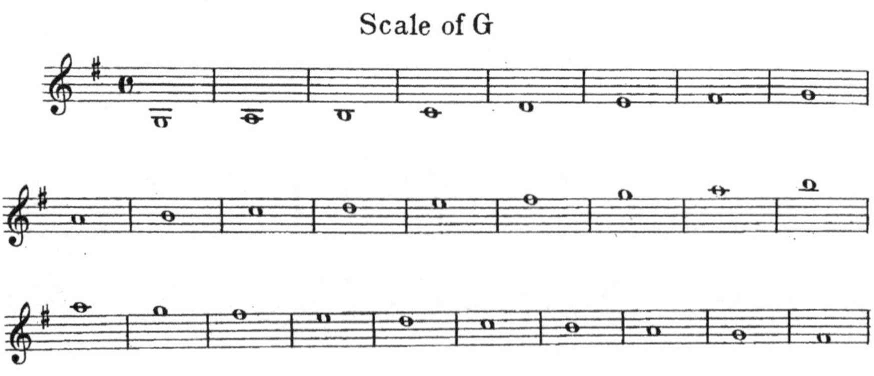

Firefly Waltz

The Tempo di Valse at the beginning means "in the time or swing of a Waltz". The "*p*" under the first measure is an abbreviation of the Italian word piano, its meaning as a musical term being "softly: gently."

The "*mf*" at the beginning of the second strain, after the double bar, stands for mezzo forte (also Italian,) meaning "half, or medium loud." Single strokes only are used in this Waltz-no tremolo.

The Use of the Fourth Finger

The use of this finger has so far been confined entirely to the E string, but its use on all the other strings is absolutely essential. While in certain places it might be a matter of choice whether the seventh fret of a string or the next higher open string were used, there are many places where the use of the fourth finger is indispensible. For Example, it is practically impossible to execute properly in keys requiring flats without the continual use of the fourth finger. The higher positions also require its use, as do rapid passages in which there would otherwise be an awkward movement of the pick. Its great importance cannot be over-estimated and the student who would be a well-rounded and efficient performer is cautioned never to avoid its use, either when it is marked in the music or when the passage could be made smoother or more effective by its use. One of the secrets of its control is to keep it always in a line with the other fingers and ready to drop at a moment's notice. The position of the hand should always be such that no change or shift has to be made when the little finger is used. Its motion, like the other fingers, must be entirely from the third joint, and while its shorter length will not allow the tip to touch the string so squarely as do the other fingers, it must be rounded as much as possible, so that the first and second joints do not "break" or bend inwards. In the following Exercises, (each two measures of which should be played not only twice, as the dots indicate, but several times), as the playing is transferred to the A, D and G strings, the outside edge of the hand is brought continually nearer the body so that when the G string is reached, the palm of the hand, at the base of the fingers, practically touches the edge of the fingerboard.

This is extremely important, and, if the thumb is held according to previous directions, will prove that the little finger is long enough to do anything that will be required of it. All fingers are to remain on the strings as long as possible.

Changing Fingers with the Up Stroke

Up to the present time, the taking of a new note has invariably come with the down stroke-an operation which requires less agility and exactness than when the note or finger changes with the stroke. For the purpose of developing a very precise and exact simultaneous movement of the hands, it is suggested that, without the instrument, the left hand be held exactly as if it were holding a pick and both hands held in front of the body, as if making a double stroke-with two picks. Both hands are now to make a quick movement like a stroke, very vigorous and at the same instant. This may be done with both the up and down movements of the hand and should be so energetic that but a single impulse is given and that there can be no discrepancy in the movements. This simultaneous movement of the hands is now to be applied to the fingerboard in the following Study, by dropping the finger on the A in the first measure at the exact moment the pick starts the up stroke. This may seem an unnecessary precaution and suggestion, but as a matter of fact the finger is quite liable to slightly precede the pick and thus cut the previous note short, or else to get to the string after the pick, in which case the note itself is spoiled. In the case of the third note (G), the first finger leaves the string at the exact moment the pick is started on its downward course, thus being entirely away from it by the time the pick gets there. The secret is in starting the movement of both hands at the same instant no matter whether the finger or pick is to go up or down. As previously explained, the action of the fingers must be very energetic and forceful. The suggestions given for the first finger and first measure apply to all the others. It is also essential that all fingers remain in position on the notes they have played so long as the playing remains on any one string. Since all notes are to be taken with down and up strokes, the use of the fourth finger in the fourth measure is necessary for the D's, since the angle of the pick would have to be changed and it would be an awkward matter to play the open D with an up stroke. This awkward crossing of the strings with an up stroke is sometimes necessary, but should not be indulged in where it can be avoided by the use of the fourth finger. The action of this finger must be particularly energetic, since it is somewhat weaker (at first) than the others, and requires special attention. In the fifth measure, since the D is to be taken with a down stroke, it would be as bad to take it on the G string as not to do so in the previous measure. All groups of four notes are to be strongly accented.

Study for Both Hands

(SPECIAL NOTE) "Eleanor Gavotte" *(Bickford)* may be used here.

Grazioso

This brisk little tune, in the style of a Polka, is a practical application of the principles explained in the previous Study. Fingers must be left on the strings as long as possible.

(SPECIAL NOTE) "Gaiety" and "Flying Birds" *(Bickford)* are suggested here.

Hasta La Manana! (man-yah-na)

This little Polka illustrates a more extended use of Accidentals, as well as of the fourth finger. The cancel in the third measure is cautionary rather than necessary, as are those in several other measures. That in the first measure, however, is necessary, as the second C is natural. The letters *"D. C."* at the end represent the Italian words Da Capo-(from the beginning,) and indicate that the player is to return to the beginning of the piece and play as far as the sign 𝄐 placed over the double bar. This sign is called a HOLD when it is placed over a double bar or a note, and a PAUSE when it is placed over a rest. Its use over the double bar is to indicate the end or close of the composition, this also being indicated by the word FINE. Either one or both may be used, at the discretion of the composer. *D. C. al* 𝄐 thus means to play from the beginning to the Hold or Fine. The two measures at the end in brackets are "endings," the first being played when the strain is played the first time, but the second only, when the strain is repeated. This is indicated by the figures in the brackets. (The proper pronunciation of the foreign words used in music is given in the Dictionary of Musical Terms at the end of the book, and it is suggested that the student pay careful attention to this feature, since mis-pronounced Musical Terms are-at the very least-not a sign of erudition!)

(Special Note - This may be studied at a later period at the descretion of the teacher.)

Scale Study in G

※NOTE: In descending passages like this, the first finger must always remain firmly on its note until after the fourth finger has been placed on the next string. This also applies to other fingers than the first.

G String Etude

Half Notes

Half notes are similar in shape to the whole note, with the addition of a stem, which, as with all notes, can be turned either up or down from the note-head.

Half notes are just half the length of whole notes, each being given <u>two beats</u>. The curved lines extending over each four measures are <u>slurs</u>, and are used to indicate the <u>phrasing</u> or division of the melody into little sentences or sections.

During the course of the phrase or slur, there is to be no break in the tremolo, but there must be a slight break, corresponding to a comma or the taking of a breath in reading, at the end of a slur, each new phrase being begun with a slight accent or emphasis.

Careful attention to the phrasing, as indicated by the slurs, marks the difference between musicianly playing and the mere haphazard throwing together of a succession of notes. Phrasing makes a melody say something. The occasional use of the fourth finger is to make the flow of the melody smoother by avoiding the crossing of strings and by keeping the same quality of tone by remaining as long as possible on one string.

Tremolo Melody

(SPECIAL NOTE) "Idly Dreaming" *(Bickford)* may be used here.

Starting and Stopping the Tremolo

As previously explained, the tremolo starts with a down stroke and ends with an up stroke, and in this connection it should be said that the first stroke of a tremolo should be a real stroke - coming toward the string from a little distance, rather than being laid against the string. This initial impulse gives the hand and the movement an impetus and steadiness which is difficult to attain without it.

The other extreme should not be indulged in, however, that of swinging the hand back and forth, getting "under headway," before the pick is in contact with the string. The following Example illustrates, as nearly as can be done with signs, the starting and stopping of the tremolo, the waved line indicating its continuance.

When the movement of a piece is moderately quick, and the tremolo is stopped either between two notes or at the end of a note immediately followed by a single stroke, there must be enough of a pause to allow the hand to prepare itself for the next down stroke or tremolo, as the case may be. This is usually best done by ending the tremolo with the up stroke on the last beat before the single note or the new tremolo.

Thus, in the Example below, the combined value of the first two notes being four beats, the tremolo is ended exactly on or with the first beat of the second measure. This final up stroke must not be separated in the least from those preceding it, nor must it be accented in the least, even though it appears to be on the first beat of a measure. This first beat, usually accented, has now entirely lost its aggressive character by being tied to a previous note, and merely represents the weak and unimportant end of a long note. While this final up stroke, so far as the moment of making it is concerned, is decisive, yet it must be so light and unaccented as to scarcely be heard. In the fifth measure the up stroke ending the tremolo ends in the same manner, exactly on the second beat, the same being true in the following measures. The tone during the five beats of the last two half notes must gradually die away so that it is scarcely perceptible at the final stroke. It is most essential that these final up strokes always be very light-never accented in the least. These principles are to be applied in all similar places. The dot and tie are explained on the following page.

The grace note just before the last up stroke represents the last down stroke of the tremolo. This is illustrated in detail in The Bickford Tenor Banjo Method (Carl Fischer).

When to Tremolo

It is difficult to give any definite rules as to the tremolo, except the general rule that all notes should be tremoloed which are too long to be effectively played with single strokes. It may be said that whole and half notes are always played with the tremolo, while those of shorter duration frequently require it, but more often do not. This seeming discrepancy is owing to the fact that the tempo or movement of a piece varies, according to its character, so that a quarter note, under certain conditions, is held as long as a half note under other conditions.

The application of this rule requires another, equally important-that single strokes must always be used when the notes are too short to admit of an effective use of the tremolo. The taste and judgment of the performer is thus called upon to decide when to use the tremolo and when not to use it. Suggestions from time to time, however, will keep the student from forming pernicious habits in this regard. While the slur frequently calls for the tremolo, it does not always do so, and does not indicate the tremolo.

Prolonging Notes or Rests

The regular value of notes may be increased by the use of a dot and by means of the tie. The dot adds one half to the value of the note, thus in reality being an abbreviation of the

Prolonging Notes or Rests *(continued)*

note next smaller in denomination. The tie, a curved line connecting two notes on the same degree of the staff, combines these two notes into one long note having the value of both. The following Example illustrates both the dot and the tie, and shows that they equal each other, in these instances.

Rests are affected by the dot in the same manner as notes.

"Music is to the mind as air is to the body." PLATO

The Importance of Leaving the Left Hand Fingers in Position

The importance of this rule cannot be over-estimated, since it has more to do with the proper technical development of the fingers, the clarity and distinctness of the tones and the general musical effect than perhaps any other one thing.

As previously stated, the fingers never rest on the frets, but rather, back of and against them-not merely between them, but against that fret which produces the desired note or pitch. The fingers must always be dropped with force-not merely laid or pressed against the strings-and must remain firmly in position as long as possible, that is, until needed elsewhere. Some of the advantages of leaving fingers down are: first, that any finger held down acts as a guide for the following note. Second, rapid runs, grace notes, trills, etc., are made practicable only by the application of this rule. Third, it leads to the easy mastery of all chords and double note passages. Fourth, it makes for ease and neatness in playing, since it often saves unnecessary raising and dropping of the fingers. Contrary to the system adopted in some Methods (violin as well as mandolin) of indicating by an "x", or a thin or dotted line, the length of time the fingers may remain in position, the author recommends that the habit be formed from the start, so that it is the natural thing to leave the fingers in position, without the aid of reminders.

Fourth Finger Study

"Any fool can play a finger exercise, but it takes a wise man to adapt what he has learned from playing such an exercise to the uses of his interpretative work." ERNEST HUTCHESON

Fundamental Rules for Picking

It is a fundamental fact, demonstrated by the ease with which a body or thing of any size falls or drops, compared with its utter inability to raise itself alone, that the down stroke is easier to make and better adapted by its nature to make accents than the up stroke. This law is recognized and utilized in the bowing of the violin, and must be in picking the mandolin. Since all rules have exceptions, these must be taken as general rules-to be followed when possible.

1. The down stroke begins all measures, all groups of notes, and plays all accented notes. This rule is extended to embrace all beats or counts, whether accented or not, and even half beats (eighth notes in 2/4 time.)

2. Only such notes as are too rapid to come under Rule 1 are played with alternating down and up strokes, the principal use of the up stroke, as applied to single notes or strokes, being to facilitate the execution in rapid passages or notes.

(In this connection it is interesting to note that the original Spanish Students who played the bandurria, never used the up stroke, except in the tremolo, their wrists having been trained to a wonderful degree of rapidity in the use of down strokes).

3. When changing from one string to another, the first note on the new string must be taken with a down stroke. This rule is emphasized by all the great representatives of the Italian School of playing, which is the logical method of playing the mandolin, as distinguished from those Schools or methods of playing which have merely adapted the down-up method of violin bowing to the right hand on the mandolin, regardless of its real adaptability. With the pick held at the proper angle the up stroke is inconvenient when changing strings, this being a sufficient reason for avoiding its use, when possible.

There are many exceptions to these rules-all of which will be taken up as they occur in the course of the work. The important thing is to make them fundamental habits.

In the Springtime

Waltz

The previous rules given for the phrasing apply throughout this little Waltz.
Quarter notes are not tremoloed in Waltzes, except in unusual cases which will be noted later.

There is a slight pause or break in the tremolo (not in the time) at the end of the fourth measure, but that at the end of the eighth measure is more noticeable. These are comparable to a comma and a semi-colon.

All stops of the tremolo (see fifth measure) are to be made as previously explained.

The Tremolo in 2/4 Time

The following Example illustrates the manner of stopping the tremolo in 2/4 time and also which notes are to be tremoloed. The first two measures are of course exactly alike in effect, the up stroke ending the tremolo exactly with the beginning of the second beat, while in the third measure the tremolo (which is stopped between the notes for the purpose of accent) stops on the "and" in each case, as it does in the fourth measure. This illustrates the correct manner of playing Marches, One Steps, Polkas, Galops, etc., most of which are written in 2/4 time.

The Juggler March

This March is to be played in a lively, Martial style, all the beats being strongly accented and with the tremolo used as described in the previous Example. The first four measures are called the Introduction, since they serve to introduce the regular melody beginning at the fifth measure. The last strain is to be repeated, the two endings being used, as previously explained. *f*, under the first measure, stands for *forte* meaning loud, forceful.

D. S. al Fine indicates a return to the Sign at the end of the Introduction and playing from there to the Fine at the end of the first strain. The word "to" is frequently used in place of al, as is also the sign 𝄐, in place of Fine.

"The Student should continually examine his own work with the same acuteness he would be expected to show, were he teaching another." JOSEF HOFFMAN

My First Duet

In this and all succeeding duets, indicated by the joining of two staves, the pupil is to play the upper part only, the second part being played by the teacher or an advanced player. Particular attention must be given to the counting and the phrasing, as well as to a smooth, soft tremolo.

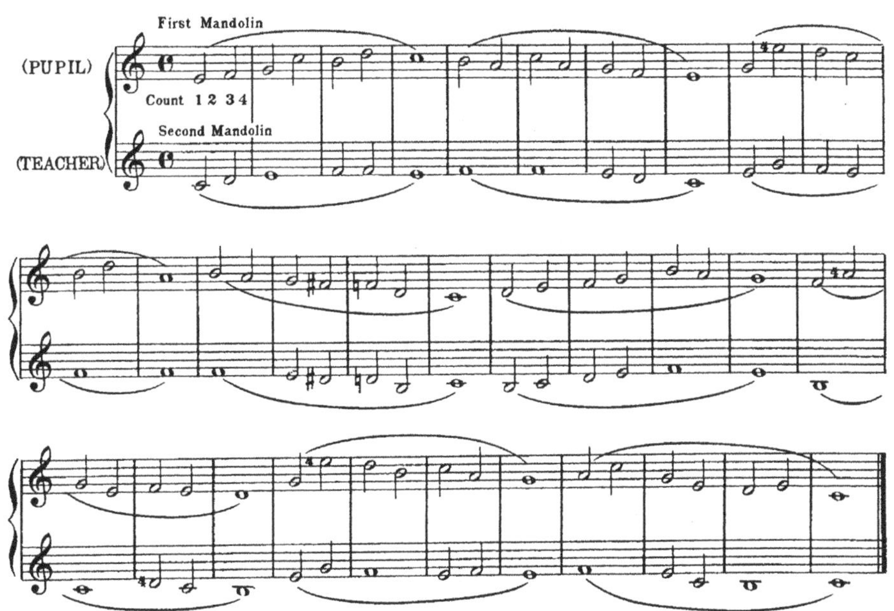

Repeating the Same Note when Tremoloed

When the same note is repeated during a tremolo passage the left hand has a duty to perform, as well as the right. The tremolo must be stopped for an instant, but at the same time, the grip of the left hand finger on the string is loosened, so that, during the short interval in which the pick is away from the string, the string itself is away from the fret. This is accomplished by letting up on the pressure of the finger so that the string barely leaves the fret against which it has been pressed, but the finger itself does not leave the string. This stops the vibrations of the string, so that there is an actual separation or articulation of the consecutive notes or tones. This is a most essential item in artistic playing and must be carefully watched. In the case of a repeated note on an open string, the vibrations are stopped by touching the string very lightly with the first finger, during the interval when the pick is away from the string, being careful not to press the string down so that it touches one of the frets, since this would defeat the object. These rules must be applied whenever there is an opportunity.

La Chacha

Waltz

This Waltz illustrates the repeated note, in the second and third measures, and also introduces the dotted quarter note, followed by an eighth, in the second part. The dot adds the value of an eighth note, the second beat of the measure coming on the dot, while the following eighth is the last half of the beat ("and").

"Call in sweet music. I have heard soft airs can charm our senses and expel our cares."
SIR J. DENHAM

The Talking Doll

This amusing little tune introduces a form of composition called "imitation", and also a free use of rests, which must be carefully watched.

Intervals

An interval is the difference in pitch between two tones, taking its name from the number of letters it includes. Thus, from C to C is a prime, C to D, a second, etc.

The following table shows the intervals as far as tenths, larger intervals usually being reckoned as the same letters were in the first octave, an eleventh being reckoned as a fourth, etc. More extended work on the intervals at this stage is not deemed necessary, since the various intervals are constantly occurring in the Studies and Pieces. It is suggested that the intervals be memorized, and that it be borne in mind that they are named in the same manner, regardless of what letters are used. To illustrate this, the interval from E up to C is a sixth, the same as from C to A, as shown in the Example.

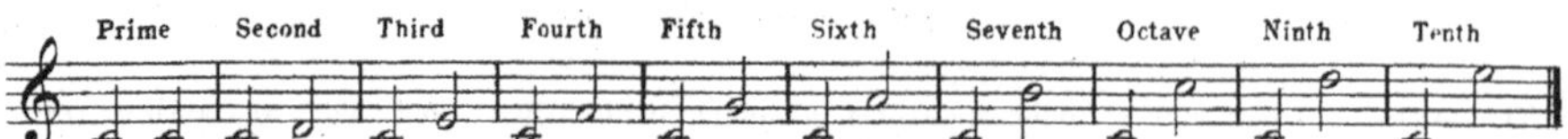

Since the primary object of this Method is to show how to play the mandolin, it is manifestly impossible to give the theory of music the attention the subject merits, consequently the student is strongly advised to procure some standard work on the subject, such as Logier's Comprehensive Course in Music and to make a thorough study of the real structure and grammar of music, which of course includes the building of chords and the formation of the intervals, major, minor, perfect, imperfect, augmented and diminished.

Moderato in G

Moderato means at a moderate rate of speed, neither too fast nor too slow. The rhythm is kept steady by the continuous quarter note figure in the second mandolin part.

"Have you real talent-real feeling for art? Then study music-do something worthy of the art-and dedicate your whole soul to the beloved saint." **LONGFELLOW**

Maypole Waltz

The second mandolin part gives the effect of a guitar and this makes a very effective little number. The solo part in the third and fourth measures must be carefully watched, the third finger being compelled to change directly across the strings.

This must be done without lifting the finger more than is necessary to place it securely on the A. In crossing strings during a continuous tremolo passage, the position of the right hand is shifted slightly so as to reach the other string, without breaking the tremolo in the least. Watch the phrasing.

p
mf
1
2

Exercise for Stopping the Tremolo

The same principle is followed in this as in previous Examples, the tremolo being stopped with the up stroke and exactly on the beat preceding the single stroke.

The reason for not ending the tremolo on the quarter note beginning the second measure, for example, with a down stroke, is that this note must not be accented, since as an individual note it does not exist, it being but the fifth beat of a whole note, in this case and very unimportant rhythmically.

Niñon (neen-yon)

This little duet for mandolin and guitar will be found very effective, but in the absence of a guitar, the accompaniment can be played on the mandolin. It is to be played rather quickly, although not like a March.

Mandolin

mf

Guitar

Expression

This is a general term referring to the intelligent, appreciative performance of music in such a manner as to bring out its inner meaning.

Thus, to play "with expression" is to follow strictly the directions of the composer, as indicated by the marks of expression, and, in the absence of these, or within the bounds of good taste and judgment, to supply or add to them from one's own originality. A composition is a musical picture, and, like any other picture, must have its lights and shades, else its soul and inner meaning will be entirely lost.

The following are some of the simpler forms of expression, with their indications, and they are to be thoroughly learned and followed in the playing.

By common consent and usage throughout the world, musical terms are written in the Italian language, the proper pronunciation of which will be found in the Musical Dictionary at the end of the book.

Animato - with life and animation.

Andante - going moderately, a somewhat slow movement.

Allegro - a quick movement.

A tempo - in time; returning to the original time.

Cantabile - in a graceful, singing style.

Crescendo - gradually increasing in strength or power. *(cresc. or* <*)*

Dolce - sweetly, softly.

Diminuendo - gradually diminishing or decreasing in volume. *(dim. or* >*)*

Decrescendo - same as above.

Forte - loud, forceful. *(f)*

Fortissimo - very loud. *(ff)*

Mezzo - half way, medium. (as mezzo-forte, mezzo-piano) *(mf - mp)*

Piano - softly, gently. *(p)*

Pianissimo - very softly. *(pp,*

Rallentando - slackening the speed, growing slower. *(rall.)*

Ritardando - (Ritenuto - same as Rallentando). *(rit.)*

Such marks as have to do with tempo or rate of movement, are controlled by the counting, but all those relating to dynamics (gradations of power or intensity), are necessarily controlled by the manner in which the pick is used. Thus, for loud tones, the pick must be held tighter and more force used in the strokes than for soft tones, the intermediate degrees being produced by the proper change in the manner of holding and using the pick. After correct intonation or pitch and well-defined rhythm, the intelligent use of dynamics (ranging from soft to loud) is the first essential toward the expressive rendering of music, since the contrasts and the very degrees of power themselves have a direct effect upon the imagination and the emotions. To ignore these means of expression is to imitate the hand organ.

Valse Petite

GURLITT

"The greater the advances we make in art the less we are satisfied with our work of an early date."
BEETHOVEN

When to Tremolo Quarter Notes

In movements where the rhythmic or martial element is less prominent and especially when the movement is too slow to make single strokes effective, quarter notes and even those of shorter duration, are played with the tremolo. This produces a more smooth and flowing effect than would the single strokes and permits the phrasing to be more carefully indicated. The term LEGATO is used to indicate a close binding together of the consecutive tones of a composition, each tone sounding until its vibra tions are stopped by the next tone. This manner of playing is indicated by the slur (also used to in dicate the phrasing), and, when the rate of speed or the character of the composition will allow it, the tre - molo is used, but the use of the slur does not necessarily indicate the tremolo, since it is perfectly possible, and indeed should be one of the chief ambitions of a performer, to play legato when using single strokes. For the purpose of forming correct habits, when quarter notes are to be played with single strokes in this work, they will be so marked in the first few measures, the absence of the stroke marks, especially if it is a legato passage and the tempo admits of it, indicating that the tremolo is to be used.

A Suggestion

While the mechanical process used in making the tremolo is practically the same as that employed in playing rapid single notes or strokes, it is necessary to get a different "feeling" or viewpoint. When single notes are played to each stroke of the pick, there is a certain mental impulse given to each note, since each stroke has a definite duty to perform in the rhythmical make-up of the measure. In the tremolo, however, the feeling must be more as though a velvet-covered pick were being used and the string gently rubbed or perhaps lightly polished. This feeling or mental picture will assist in making a smooth, even and continuous movement of the hand and consequently, the sustained tone from the string which is the object of the tremolo. The hand and pick must go through the same motions (except that there is not time to make the strokes as long), but there must not be the accent and definite mental impulse for each stroke that is necessary when playing single notes. The pick must be held very loosely and only the very tip allowed to touch the strings.

A Study in Sostenuto

The Key of D

When D is taken as the key note or starting point of the scale, it becomes necessary to retain the F sharp used in the key of G and to add C sharp, in order to bring the steps and half steps in the proper order. The important thing to remember in this key, therefore, is that every F and C is sharped. In the following Scale Study the new sharp is indicated in parenthesis. The Technical Study is to be thoroughly practiced and played at a lively pace, particular attention being paid to the use of the fourth finger. The two sharps at the beginning of the staff are the sign or signature of the key of D. Speed is attained by thinking in groups, rather than in single notes.

"Study only the best, for life is too short to study everything." P. EMANUEL BACH

Tender Thoughts

This little song with a guitar accompaniment introduces the tremolo on eighth notes, every note throughout being played with the tremolo. Particular attention must be paid to the marks of expression and the phrasing.

(SPECIAL NOTE) "Home Sweet Home" *(Arr. by Bickford)* is suggested here.

Tremolo Study in D

Harp Echoes

The mandolin accompaniment is here intended to imitate the harp. While in a broader sense the phrases are four measures in length, there must be a slight break in the tremolo at the end of each tie, the short slur indicating the beginning of a new little phrase or idea. Through it all, however, must be the thought and feeling of the four measure "sentence."

"There is no doubt that the seed of many virtues is in such hearts as are devoted to music; those who are not touched by music I hold to be like stocks and stones." MARTIN LUTHER

Further Chord Practice

For the present, down strokes are invariably used when playing chords. A complete explanation of "Duo" or chord playing in its entirety is given in the following volumes of this Method.

(SPECIAL NOTE) "All Through The Night" *(Arr. by Bickford)* is suggested here.

Minuet

This little Minuet, by one of the famous masters of the mandolin, is an example of 3/8 time, in which the eighth note is given the beat, quarter notes consequently having <u>two</u> beats. The last note in the eighth measure is to be held about three times as long as usual, as indicated by the <u>hold</u> (𝄐). <u>Rit.</u> indicates that the time is to go gradually slower until this note is reached. The prolonged note is to be tremoloed, the tone gradually dying away toward the end, after which a <u>slight</u> pause is made and then the next measure played <u>in time,</u> as indicated above it. Attention is called to the sharp contrast in going from the fourth to the fifth measure of the second movement or strain. The first four measures are <u>very loud</u>, while the next four are <u>soft</u>, like an echo.

21735-70

The last two measures at the end of this strain are gradually made slower, the quarter note being tremoloed and allowed to die away into nothing. In the Trio, the slurred eighths are tremoloed, the tremolo ending with the up stroke just as the second note is played, the accent being entirely on the first of the two notes.

Key of B Minor

This key is the relative of D Major (requiring the same signature), and the following Scale shows the use of the proper accidentals. "Sadness" requires the tremolo on all notes, including sixteenths, owing to the very slow tempo at which it is played. It may be counted at the rate of four eighth notes to a measure.

"That mind alone whose every thought is rhythm can embody music, can comprehend its mysteries, its divine inspirations, and can alone speak to the senses of its intellectual revelations!" ***BEETHOVEN***

Moderato in D

This interesting little duet shows that sixteenth notes are sometimes played with down strokes The first note of the group of four must receive its usual accent.

Triplets

A Triplet is a group of three notes played to a single pulse. Thus, three eighth notes in the form of a triplet (with the figure **3** over or under them), are equal to and are played in the time of a quarter note. The subjoined table gives the triplets in common use, with the notes they equal. In playing and counting them, they should be considered as equalling a single word with three syllables, as "Reg-u-lar," with the strong accent on the first note, the same as the first syllable.

When triplets are picked (not tremoloed), they are usually played down-up-down, each group being played in exactly the same manner. It is occasionally necessary to vary this rule when crossing strings or when the tempo is very rapid.

When two or more groups of triplets follow each other, there must not be the slightest break between the groups, the succession of strokes being like the word "reg-u-lar-reg-u-lar," in more than one sense. The slur is sometimes used in connection with 3, but is not necessary.

Triplet Etude

"Mannerism is displeasing in the original, to say nothing of the same faults in copyists." ***SCHUMANN***

Tripping !

Triplets in Quick Time

While triplets and beats should be started with down strokes, as a rule, unless tremoloed, it is occasionally necessary to break the rule, as in the following Examples. Each triplet must be slightly accented, regardless of the stroke.

Unusual Picking

It is frequently desirable to use the glide, or sliding pick, in order to avoid an awkward position or movement. For example, if the picking marked under the first measure were used, there would be an awkward crossing of the strings with the pick which is to be avoided when possible. The picking marked over the notes requires an up stroke for an occasional accent, but this is not impossible, although unusual.

The important thing in using the coulé or glide is to see that the finger does not remain on the lower string after the pick has left it, since this would cause the slurred effect which is the reason advanced by some Methods for not using this movement of the pick. However, the slur and the blur are entirely caused by the left hand and the first two notes in the following Exercise, for example, can be played as detached or staccato as is desired by merely removing the pressure of the finger on the D string at the proper moment. Exercises for the training of the right hand in making awkward strokes will be introduced at a later period.

"Everything does credit to the player which is well played." CZERNY

Grace Notes

The Grace Note is more frequently used than any of the other "Musical Ornaments", its use adding greatly to the beauty of a melody. The common form of the grace note is technically known as the acciacatura, meaning "to crush", and thus indicating the manner in which a grace note is to be played-literally crushed against or blended with the following or principal note. The grace note is a small note with an eighth or sixteenth note stem crossed by a line or stroke, and having no defined time or length.

It is to be played as quickly as possible and usually steals the necessary time from the following note. An older form of the grace note (called the appoggiatura) was written in the form of a small note representing half the length of the following note and taking this much time from the principal note. This form frequently occurs in the works of Haydn, Mozart, and other famous masters of the past. The modern grace note is frequently called the short appoggiatura. In the first of the following Examples, the tremolo is started on the grace note, as though that were the only note to be played, it being given the first count or beat-but the finger is immediately dropped on the string for the following note, without any break in the tremolo or the connection of the notes. The tremolo, as usual, is to be started with a slight accent and the finger should be on the principal note by the time the second (up) stroke of the tremolo is played, thus making the value of the grace note that of one stroke of the tremolo-extremely short. In the second Example, the grace note, being on another string, is executed by starting the tremolo with the down stroke in the same manner, but allowing the first stroke to slide quickly over two strings, thus really making the grace note like the lower note of a chord.

The third Example shows the double grace note, in which the tremolo starts on the first grace note, the second being taken with the second stroke (the up stroke) of the tremolo, while the principal note comes on the third stroke of the continuous tremolo movement. The important thing is to start these little notes as though they were the only notes to be played, the impulse or beat starting with the grace note. The main accent must come on the principal note, but this note is to be reached so quickly after the initial impulse is started that there is no perceptible time given to the grace note or notes. According to the greatest authorities, from Philip Emanuel Bach, (son of the immortal Bach) down to Grove's Dictionary of Music, Louis C. Elson, and many others, the time of the grace note, small as it is, is always taken from the principal or following note. Grove says: "It (the grace note) consists in suspending or delaying a note of a melody by means of a note introduced before it; the time required for its performance, whether long or short, being always taken from the principal note." Originally grace notes were invariably written a step or a half step away from the principal note, thus being actually suspensions or delayed progressions of the melody note. Since grace notes must begin on the beat (in piano playing with the bass or accompaniment), it will be of assistance to compare the single grace note to a word of two syllables, like "suc-ceed", in which the accent is entirely on the last syllable. To speak this word quickly requires but a single impulse, this impulse of course being started with the first syllable (corresponding to the grace note), but culminating on the last syllable (corresponding to the principal note). The double grace note can be compared to a three-syllabled word like "in-ter-cede", in which the accent also falls on the last syllable, the first two syllables corresponding to the two grace notes, while the last syllable corresponds to the principal note. The word must be spoken very quickly and with but a single impulse or thrust in order to get the comparison. In a broad sense, grace notes embrace all the various ornaments or embellishments used to adorn and beautify a melody, such as the Mordent, the Turn or Grupetto and the Trill. Modern usage, however, confines the term entirely to the small notes, as explained above.

※(See note at bottom of page)

※ NOTE: The tremolo and vibration of the string must be stopped before the grace note is started, otherwise there will be no grace note. This applies to all of the places marked on this page and in all similar cases.

Study for Both Hands

This little Study is to be played as quickly as possible, using the fourth finger wherever indicated and making the fingers of the left hand feel the rhythm of each note and in this manner work exactly with the pick. A single impulse for both hands. The first note of each group is to be strongly accented.

"A good rhythm indicates a finely balanced musician-one who knows how and one who has perfect self-control. All the book study in the world will not develop it." KATHERINE GOODSON

(SPECIAL NOTE) "On The Way" *(Bickford)* is suggested here.

Patricia Waltz

This little Waltz can be accompanied by either a second mandolin (playing the small notes on the upper staff), or a guitar, or both, thus making a TRIO. The large notes at the top, with the stems turned up, are for the solo part. The third movement or section of a composition is called the TRIO, thus giving the word a different meaning than when it refers to three players.

p
1
2
mf
Fine
1
2

Patricia Waltz *(continued)*

Studies in Chord Playing

These short Studies are for the purpose of developing the ability to change quickly from one chord position to another-without the slightest break in the time.

The left hand fingering must be followed closely, some of the notes having to be taken with un usual fingers. In quick movements like these, it is necessary to use more of a real stroke or swing of the right hand than is the case in slower tempos.

The two, three or four notes of the chord are to sound practically as though struck on the piano.

"Music's a great and never-failing treasure to those who've learnt and studied it in youth." THEOPHILUS.

Simple and Compound Time

Simple time is that which has one note for a beat unit, as 2/4, 3/4 and 4/4, in which the quarter note is the beat or unit, also 3/8 and 4/8, in which the eighth note is the beat note. Compound time is the kind of time which has a triplet, or something that will equal it, on each beat, and is used for the purpose of avoiding the writing of triplets. In all compound times the lower figure indicates the notes of which the triplets are formed, while the upper figure, when divided by three (the number of notes forming a triplet), will give the number of beats or pulses to the measure. The compound times are indicated by the following signatures:- 6/8, 6/4, 9/8 and 12/8. The following Examples show how the same passage may be written in either simple or compound time, the effect being exactly the same in both cases. In the 6/8 time, the beat, which in itself is the same as in 2/4 time, has to be represented by a dotted quarter, since it must equal the three eighth notes of the triplet.

Thus it happens that the half note in 2/4 time equals the dotted half note in 6/8 time. Since the beat note is the same in the three kinds of compound time here shown (the dotted quarter note), 9/8 time equals 3/4 time and 12/8 equals Common time.

In the last measure of the 12/8 time, the dots following the eighth note and the eighth rest represent the value of a sixteenth note and rest.

When the movement is very slow, as in the "Melody" below, it is allowable to count six eighth notes to a measure, giving a strong accent, however, to the first and fourth beats, since these beats begin the two groups of triplets which really comprise the measure.

Melody in 6/8 Time

(SPECIAL NOTE) "Aloha Oe" *(Arr. by Bickford)* is suggested here.

Playing 2/4 Time

The following table shows the correct manner of picking the various figures and combinations of groups which ordinarily appear in Galops, Polkas, One Steps, Two Steps, Marches and other dances which may be written in this time. These figures should be memorized so that there is never any hesitation as to what strokes to use when similar passages occur. There will be occasional exceptions, but they will be so obvious as not to be confusing.

Two Steps and Marches in 6/8 Time

All quick movements in this kind of time are to be picked and considered as though the eighth notes were triplets-that is, each group of three notes to be played down-up-down, all quarter notes to be single down strokes and all dotted quarters and longer notes to be tremoloed. The following short Example gives an idea of the movement, the lower staff showing that by taking down strokes on the same parts of the measure as though it were all played in eighth notes, the picking and accents will be uniform.

The effect of the first two measures in the lower staff is the same, although the notes appear to be of different lengths. Sixteenths must be played down-up.

If necessary, this exercise and the following March may be counted six to a measure, during the first practice.

Example in 6/8 Time

In Martial Mood

Short Study

"Those who think that music ranks among the trifles of existence are in gross error."
WILLIAM E. GLADSTONE

The Metronome

This is a little instrument invented by Maelzel in 1816 for marking or measuring the time. Its principal use is to indicate the rate of movement desired by the composer, although it can also be made to assist in developing a sense of rhythm by listening carefully to the regular ticks and endeavoring to imitate them in the counting or beating. The figures on the face of the dial show the number of ticks it will give per minute with the top of the little sliding weight set at any given figure.

The letters M. M. stand for "Maelzel's Metronome," the figures frequently given at the beginning of a composition, immediately following a note, indicating the rate at which these particular notes are to be played. Thus, (♪= 60) indicates that eighth notes are to be played at the rate of 60 to the minute, or one to a second, the top of the little weight being set at 60 on the dial. There is also a form of the instrument in the shape of a little pocket tape measure, and the use of one or the other is strongly advised, although the real development of the sense of rhythm must come from within.

The pocket metronome and its use are more fully explained in a later volume.

O'er Hill and Dale

Polka-March

This March changes the key in the Trio, from G to C (no sharps). When going back to the beginning, as indicated by the D. C. at the end, second endings only are to be played, this being always understood among musicians, but seldom indicated.

This is to be played with two strong accents to the measure, allowing the swing of the hand to mark the time in making the strokes.

f
pp
mp
f
ff
mf
1
2
Fine
pp-f (loud when repeating)
1
2
D. C. al Fine

Chord Studies

The following Chord Studies will be found to have more difficult combinations of the fingers than those previously given. Fingers used for the single notes are to be retained for the measure of chords in every case.

Chromatic Study

The left hand fingers must slide quickly and easily from one fret to the next. The occasional use of <u>flats</u> will be noticed.

"The first and most indispensable quality of any artist is to feel respect for great men, and to bow down in spirit before them; to recognize their merits, and not to endeavor to extinguish their great flame in order that his own feeble rushlight may burn a little brighter." MENDELSSOHN

Dotted Eighth Notes

The dot after an eighth note adds the value of a sixteenth note, thus being an abbreviation of the sixteenth. This is shown in the first two measures of the first Example below, which sound and are played exactly the same. Like all tied notes, the first of the two sixteenths in the first measure is held or waited for, but not played again, the same being true of the dot in the following measure. It will be seen that the dotted eighth is exactly three times as long as the sixteenth which follows it, thus (if two be counted to the measure) using up exactly three-quarters of a beat-which is practically the whole beat in a moderately quick tempo. The exact division is easy to make if the counting is very slow, but in quick tempos it becomes necessary to think of the dotted note, not only as the important part, but as practically the whole of the beat, connecting the sixteenth note with the following note, both mentally and actually, almost as though it were a grace note and written with the next note. This manner of picturing the sixteenth note can perhaps be illustrated as being counted-"one--n'two--n'three--n'four," as distinguished from the exact division of "one-and-two," etc. The beat itself (dotted note) must be held practically until it is time to play and count the next beat (dotted note), the sixteenth not being considered as having any time at all, although theoretically it has a quarter of the beat. A careful application of this rule will develop the style of playing which distinguishes the expert from the novice-the artist from the artisan.

It should be added that the real effect of a dotted note passage in quick tempos is and usually should be as though there were a rest in place of the dot, as illustrated in Example 4.

Toujours Gai

The Mazurka is an original Polish Dance, somewhat slower than the modern Waltz, but with the rhythm and accents strongly marked. Since the tendency of the tremolo is to smooth over, rather than to bring out strong accents and contrasts, it is usually best to confine it strictly to half notes, the same as in Waltzes. The characteristic feature of a Mazurka is the strong accent on the second beat, as well as on the first.

It is necessary in this piece to return to the beginning, playing the first strain once through, before as well as after playing the Trio.

(SPECIAL NOTE) "Shambling Sam" (*Bickford*) is suggested here.

Key of F

Starting the scale on F requires the use of B flat, all the other tones being natural, as in the key of C. While the signature is B flat, the key is F. The picking, as indicated in the Scale, is to be carefully followed. In the Melody, the division into two-measure phrases or sentences is to be carefully followed, but, in the larger melodic sense, the entire piece is divided into a question and answer, each being eight measures in length and closing with the whole note.

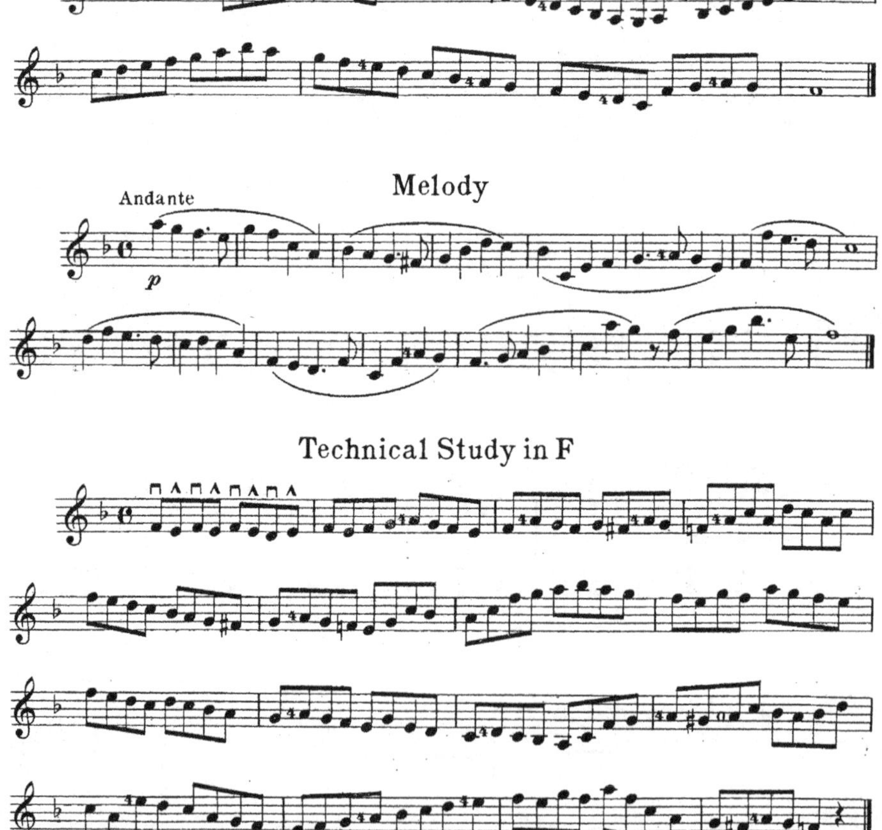

"You will not take music lessons all your life. Work therefore every day to make yourself as independent as possible." *WILLIAM MASON*

In Graceful Mood

Tempo di Schottische (♩= 126)

(SPECIAL NOTE) "June Days" *(Bickford)* is suggested here.

Scale of D Minor

(Relative of F Major)

"He who learns to play music in his eightieth year will play at the resurrection." TURKISH PROVERB

Extending the Fourth Finger

It is frequently necessary or advisable to extend the fourth finger beyond the seventh fret on all of the strings, since this frequently makes the picking easier, by confining the work to a single string, or by simplifying the crossing of the strings. In each of the following Examples, this finger is extended to the eighth fret, thus making the note a half step higher than the seventh fret and the next open string, the preceding finger in the meantime remaining firmly on its note.

These are to be played rather slowly and with careful attention to the fingering.

Study Introducing Fourth Finger Extension

Dance of the Honey Bugs

The guitar accompaniment to this quaint little dance will be very effective. The first strain is an adaptation of an old Southern dance, or "Walk Around."

Although there is no change of signature in the Trio, this is in the key of F Major.

This is shown by the fact that the melody or theme begins and ends on F, and that all the chords belong to the key of F instead of D Minor (which is the key of the first two strains.) The use of the fourth finger of the left hand is absolutely essential.

Key of A

When the scale starts on A, it becomes necessary to use three sharps, F, C and G, to maintain the proper order of intervals, as explained in the C scale. This is indicated by the signature at the beginning of the staff. The Scale should be thoroughly practiced, using the tremolo throughout.

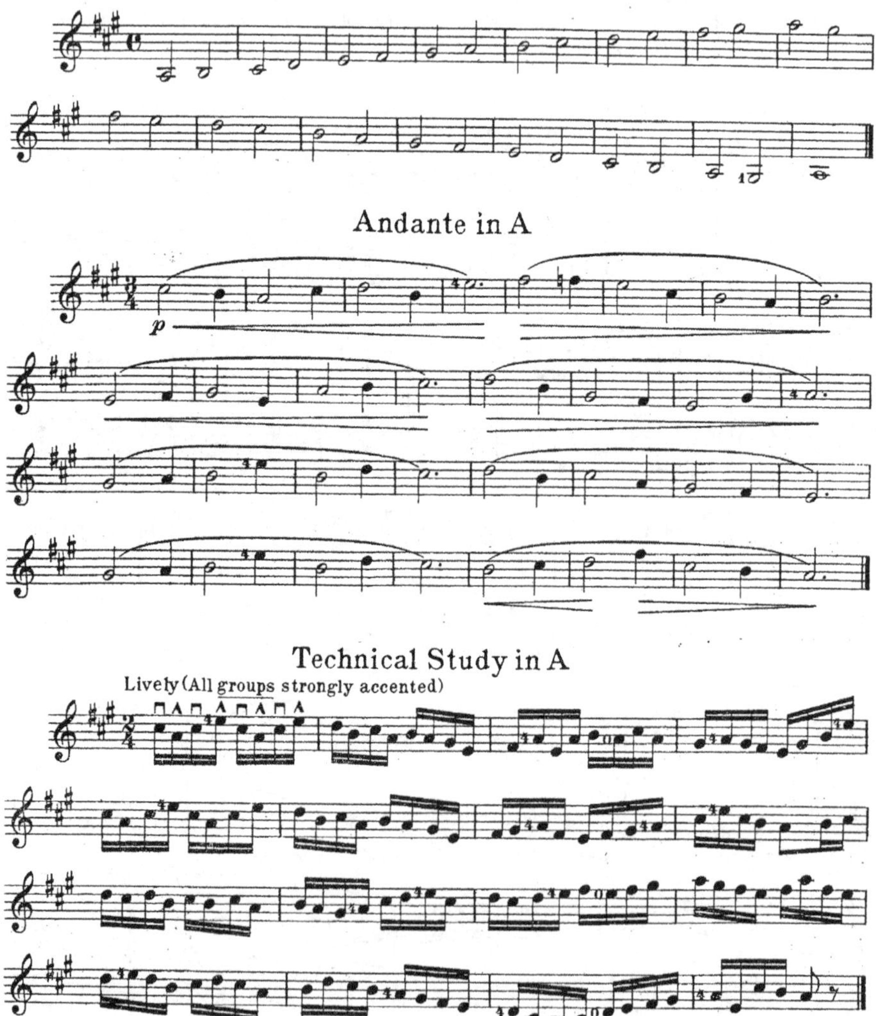

LIST OF MUSICAL TERMS
With their proper pronunciation

Accelerando (at-chel-leh-rahń-do) - gradually quickening the time.
Adagio (ah-dah-jeo) - a slow movement; slower than Andante.
Ad libitum (ad lib-y-tum) - at the will or pleasure of the performer.
Acciaccatura (ah-chee-ah-kah-toó-rah) - a short grace note, taking its time from the following note.
Alla Breve (ah-lah bray-veh) - two half notes to the measure.
Allegretto (ahl-lay-gret-to) - a little slower than *Allegro*.
Allegro (ahl-lay-gro) - quick, lively; a quick movement. Frequently modified by other words.
Amateur (ahm-ah-ter) - a lover of art; not a professional.
Andante (ahn-dahń-teh) - a slow, quiet movement, often modified by other words.
Andantino (ahn-dahn-teé-no) - a diminutive of *andante*, hence *should* mean "going a little less" (a little slower), but commonly interpreted as a little faster than (*andante*.
Animato (ahn-y-mah-toh) - lively; with animation.
Appoggiatura (ah-podg-ee-ah-toó-rah) - a grace note having two forms - *long* and *short*.
Arpeggio (are-pedǵ-ee-oh) - the tones of a chord performed in succession rather than simultaneously.
A tempo (ah tem-po) - in time; denotes a return to the original time, or movement.
Bandurria (bahn-doó-ree-ah) - a Spanish type of the mandolin.
Barré (bar-ray) - crossing or stopping two or more strings with a single finger.
Baton (baa-ton(gh) - a stick used for beating time.
Ben (behn) - well, or strongly. Used with other words.
Bis (beess) - twice.
Bravura (brah-voó-rah) - boldness; brilliancy.
Break (brake) - a term applied to the two measures sometimes played at the close of a dance to indicate that the music is to stop.
Berceuse (behr-serze) - a lullaby or cradle song.
Cadenza (kah-dehń-tsah) - an ornamental passage frequently introduced into compositions.
Cantabile (kahn-tah-bee-leh) - in a smooth, singing manner; with expression.
Capo tasto (káh-po tahs-to) - }
Capo dastro (kah-po dahs-tro) - } a movable nut or clamp used to shorten the strings of a fretted instrument.
Capriccio (kah-prit-chee-oh) - in a capricious, whimsical style.
Con (konn) - with. Used with other words.
Coda (kó-dah) - a few measures added for a more effective close.
Concerto (kohn-chehr-to) - a composition designed to display the capabilities of an instrument, accompanied by an orchestra or other instrument.
Coulé (koo-lay) - as applied to mandolin playing, the sliding of the pick from one string to another without being raised between.
Crescendo (kreh-shen-do) - increasing in loudness.
Crochet (krotch-et) - the English term for a quarter note.
Cued Notes - the small notes indicating the part being played by another instrument.
Da Capo (dah kah-po) - from the beginning (to the word *Fine* or the 𝄐).
Dal Segno (dahl sané-yo) - from the *sign* (𝄋)
Decrescendo (day-kreh-shen-do) - gradually decreasing in power.
Delicato (del-ee-kah-to) - delicately, smoothly.
Diminuendo (dy-min-oo-eń-do) - diminishing; same as *decrescendo*.
Dolce (dolé-cheh) - softly, sweetly.
Divisi (dee-veé-szee) - divided, as between two players or sets of players.
Doublet - a pulse divided into two parts. Used in 6/8 and other compound times.
Elegante (el-ay-gahń-teh) - with elegance and grace.
Ensemble (ahn (g)-sahmbl) - together; the union of several performers: also the effect of the combination.
Encore (ahn(g)-core) - again; more.
Energico (en-ehŕ-jee-ko) - energetic, vigorous.
Entr'acte (ahn (g)-trahkt) - between the acts; music played between acts of a drama.
Espressivo (es-pres-seé-vo) - with expression.
Etude (ay-teeud, almost *ay-tood*) - a *musical study* as distinguished from an *exercise*.
Finale (fee-nah-leh) - the final movement.
Fine (feé-neh) - the end.
Forte (foré-teh) - loud.
Fortissimo (fore-tisś-see-mo) - very loud.
Forza (fort-sah) - force, power.
Fuoco (foo-oh-ko) - fire; passion; impetuosity.
Galop (gal-o) - a lively dance in 2/4 time.
Glissando (glis-sahń-do) - sliding the fingers from one fret to another.
Grazioso (graht-see-ó-so) - elegant, graceful.
Giusto (joos-to) - just, strict, correct.
Grandioso (grahn-dee-ó-so) - grandeur, dignity.
Grave (grah-veh) - slow, solemn.

Gusto (goos̕-to) - taste, expression.
Harmony - the science of chords, their construction and progression.
Larghetto (lar-get̕-to) - slow, but not so slow as *largo*.
Lar̕-go - slowly, broadly.
Legato (leh-gah̕-to) - very closely connected; bound together.
Leggiero (led-jee-eh̕-ro) - light, rapid, delicate.
Lento (lehn̕-to) - slow.
L'istesso (lees-tes̕-so) - the same: in the same tempo.
Lo-co, as written; return to the regular pitch.
Ma non troppo (mah nohn trop̕-po) - but not too much so.
Maestoso (mah-ess-tó-so) - stately; dignified; majestic.
Marcato (mar-kah̕-to) - marked, accented.
Marcia (mar̕-chee-ah) - a march: used with *tempo di*.
Meno (may̕-no) - less. Used with other words, as *meno mosso* - less motion or speed.
Mezzo (met̕-so) - half, medium, as *mezzo forte*, midway between *piano* and *forte*.
Moderato (mode-eh-rah̕-to) - moderately: *allegro moderato* - moderately fast.
Molto (molé-to) - much, extremely: *molto allegro* - very fast.
Morendo (mo-rané-do) - dying away: gradually softer and slower.
Mos̕-so, movement or motion.
Mó-to, motion or movement. *Con moto* - with life and animation.
Non (nohn) - no, not.
Notation - the signs which represent musical tones.
Obligato ob-lee-gah̕-to) - an essential part accompanying a solo.
Opus - work or composition: used by composers to indicate the order in which works are written or published - as, Opus 1, the first work.
Os̕-sia - or else, or, otherwise.
Perdendosi (pehr-den-dó-see) - dying away.
Phrasing - the art of grouping tones into phrases so as to clearly express the musical idea.
Pianissimo (pee-ahn-is̕s-ee-mo) - very softly.
Piano (pee-áh-no) - soft, gentle.
Più (peé-oo) - more, as *più mosso* - faster.
Pizzicato (pit-see-kah̕-to) - picking the strings with the fingers instead of playing an instrument in the usual manner. Usually applied to the left hand in mandolin playing.
Pó-co, a little. Used with other words. as *poco a poco* - little by little.
Poi (pó-ee) - then. As *poi Coda* - then play the Coda.
Point d'orgue (pwan(g) d'org) - organ point: applied to the *hold* or *pause* (𝄐)
Portamento (por-tah-men̕-to) - carrying or blending one tone into the next by gliding the finger along the string.
Prestissimo (pres-tis̕s-see-mo) - as fast as possible.
Pres̕-to, quick, rapid.
Primo or Prima (preé-mo, - preé-ma) - first. *Tempo primo* - the original time or movement.
Pri-ma vis̕-ta - at first sight.
Quasi (kwá-zee) - like; in the manner or style of. *Quasi allegro* - like allegro.
Rallentando (rahl-len-tahn̕-do) - gradually slower.
Rapido (rah-peé-do) - rapid, quick.
Rapidamente (rah-peed-ah-men̕-teh) - rapidly.
Rinforzando (rin-for-tsahn̕-do) - re-inforcing; placing a strong accent on a note.
Risoluto (riz-o-loó-to) - resolutely, boldly.
Ritardando (ree-tar-dahn̕-do) - slower and slower.
Ritenuto (ree-ten-oó-to) - holding back, retarding.
Rubato (roo-báh-to) - robbed, stolen. Some tones held longer and others cut shorter in proportion. (Properly used only by *artists*.)
Sans (sahn(g) - without.
Scherzando (skehrt-sahn̕-do) - jokingly, playfully.
Scherzo (skehrt̕-so) - a piece of music written in a playful, joyous mood. A movement frequently replacing the Minuet in Symphonies and Sonatas.
Score - a copy of a work in which all parts are shown.
Segno (sané-yo) - sign. *Dal segno* - from the sign.(𝄋)
Sempre (sem̕-pray) - always.
Sentimento (sen-tee-men̕-to) - with feeling and sentiment.

Sostenuto (sos-ten-oó-to) - sustaining tones for their full duration.
Staccato (stac-kaĥ-to) - detached, cut off, separated.
Stringendo (streen-jeń-do) - hurrying the time.
Subito (soo-beé-to) - at once; quickly.
Sul (sool) - on the; upon the. *Sul G* - on the G string.
Tacet (taś-set) - Is silent, or be silent.
Teḿ-po, time. Universally used to indicate "rate of movement."
Tenuto (teh-noó-to) - sustained: held the full time.
Tutti (toó-tee) - all the performers are to take part.
Trop-po, too much. Used with other words.
Tranquillo (trahn-quil'-lo) - tranquil, quiet.
Un (oon) - a. *Un poco* - a little.
Vamp - to improvise (sometimes called *fake*) an accompaniment. Also a term applied to the short passage in songs between the Introduction and the "verse" or regular strain.
Veloce (veh-ló-cheh) - rapid: swift.
Vibrato (vee-brah-to) - vibrant, wavy tone, very effective on violin and other bowed instruments, also guitar, but not on the mandolin.
Vivace (vee-vah-cheh) - lively; with animation and vivacity. A movement between *Allegro* and *presto*.
Vivo (veé-vo) - alive; brisk.

ABBREVIATIONS

Accel.	Accelerando	*Modto.*	Moderato
Acc.	Accompaniment	*Op.*	Opus
Ad lib.	Ad libitum	*8va.*	Ottava
Allo.	Allegro	*8*	Ottava
Andte.	Andante	*p*	Piano
A tem.	A tempo	*pp*	Pianissimo
A temp.	A tempo	*ppp*	Softer than Pianissimo
Cantab.	Cantabile	*Pizz.*	Pizzicato
Cresc.	Crescendo (also <)	*Imo*	Primo (as *Tempo Imo*)
D. C.	Da Capo	*Rall.*	Rallentando
Decres.	Decrescendo (also >)	*rfz*	Rinzforzando
Dim.	Diminuendo (also >)	*Rinf.*	Rinzforzando
Div.	Divisi	*Rit.*	Ritardando
Dol.	Dolce	*Riten.*	Ritenuto
D. S.	Dal Segno	𝄋	A sign
Espress.	Espressivo	*Scherz.*	Scherzando
f	Forte	*Semp.*	Sempre
ff	Fortissimo	*sfz*	Sforzando
fff	Louder than Fortissimo	*Smorz.*	Smorzando
Graz.	Grazioso	*Sos.*	Sostenuto
Intro.	Introduction	*Sost.*	Sostenuto
Leg.	Legato (also ⁀)	*Stacc.*	Staccato
Lo.	Loco	*String.*	Stringendo
Marc.	Marcato	*Ten.*	Tenuto
M. M.	Maelzel's Metronome	*tr*	Trill
mp	Mezzo piano	*Trem.*	Tremolo
mf	Mezzo forte	*Viv*	Vivace

The use of The Pocket Standard Dictionary of Musical Terms by Oscar Coon is recommended.

Afterword

The earnest student who has given careful attention to the important principles laid down in this book will have gained a comprehensive knowledge of the fundamental principles of mandolin playing and of the study of music in its elementary stage. This is but the beginning, however, and the careful and conscientious study of the three remaining volumes of the Method is urged, these fundamental principles meanwhile being constantly kept in mind and the material in this volume, both music and text, occasionally reviewed.

The Second Book contains further elaborate explanations and illustrations of the Grace Note, a very complete explanation of Syncopation and just how to play it. Particular attention is also given to the subject of Popular Music and its proper rendition. The important study of Phrasing and Expression is thoroughly covered in a novel manner, as are also the Abbreviations and short cuts used in modern music. Various intricate strokes of the pick, such as crossing strings with an up stroke, etc., are explained, with many examples. The subject of Positions is approached in an entirely new and interesting manner, the second and third positions and the proper method of shifting being thoroughly covered.

A number of famous Violin Studies (some of them with original second mandolin or guitar parts added), together with many excerpts from the classics, are included, the author believing that the general musical taste and a familiarity with the best in musical literature should be cultivated at an early stage of progress.

Special attention is also given to the study of those keys having several flats, since this has been a neglected part of the mandolinist's education.

Chord tremolo is also thoroughly covered.

The Third Book covers most of the remaining keys and positions not previously introduced, together with all of the further *ornaments* used in music

"Duo Playing" is also thoroughly explained and illustrated, in its various styles, with the most minute directions for its complete mastery.

Many famous classics, never before set for the mandolin, are included, together with helpful hints and suggestions for the general musical and technical development.

The Fourth Book contains the last word in musical and technical development, so far as the study of the mandolin is concerned, and brings out its very highest artistic possibilities, as well as those of the performer.

Right and Left Hand Harmonics are thoroughly explained and the technical resources of the instrument, in so far as practical musical results are concerned, are practically exhausted. Special instructions for arranging music for the mandolin, particularly as regards the adapting of harmony and chords to a melody, are given, together with countless hints as to interpretation, orchestral and solo playing and general useful and practical information.

Movements from several famous Violin Concertos and other important works are included, together with excerpts from the works of Paganini, Ries, Tschaikowsky and others.

In conclusion, the author desires to bespeak as careful, conscientious and systematic a study of the remaining Volumes as he feels sure has been given to this.

Made in the USA
Monee, IL
09 December 2020

51712566R00056